# TRADITIONAL KNITTING

*from the*
## SCOTTISH AND IRISII ISLES

*With over 30 glorious designs*

EDITED BY DEBBIE BLISS

CROWN PUBLISHERS, INC
NEW YORK

## CREDITS

The Publishers would like to thank the following for their help in the production of this book: Doris and Willie Milton for their generosity, kindness and unstinting good humour; Barry Milton for his organisation and patience; Bobbie Groome; Roger Milton, Vicky McKinnon and Angus; Mr and Mrs McNair and Benjie; Will Coull; Alistair Sim; Raymond McIntosh; Jackie O'Brien; Irene Vass; Katie Baillie; Lisbet, Karina and Barbara Christensen; Julia-Jane and David Gladwin and Ted; Giles, Richard and Louise Pearson; Robert Macrae; John Donald; June and David Alexander; Doreen Davidson; Sarah Fraser; Ernie Stewart; Iain Innes and family; Douglas Dawson; Carlo Manzi Rentals for men's trousers, shirts, caps and shoes; The Scotch House for tartan trousers, kilts, shawls and scarves; B.S.C.O. for denim jeans; The Regent Belt Company for leather belts; Dan Air.

The editor would like to thank Rex Gardener and Associates for their invaluable help.
Tina Eggleton for her good humour and her endless patience and skill in checking and compiling patterns.
All the designers, knitters and companies who contributed to the book.
Sandra Lousada for her beautiful photography and Marie Willey for perfect styling.

The Editor would also like to thank the following for creating the beautiful designs that feature in this book:

**Lesley Stanfield** Aran Jacket with Blackberry Stitch *page 100* Twisted Rib Aran Sweater *page 117* 'Sampler' Style Gansey *page 69* Fair Isle Long Line Slipover *page 50* Traditional Fair Isle Sweater *page 40*
**Pat Quiroga** Yoke Pattern Gansey *page 65*
**Sheila Hollingworth** Aran Fishing Shirt *page 108*
**T.M. Adie and Sons** Man's Slipover with Fair Isle Border *page 36*
**Jamiesons Knitwear** Man's All Over Fair Isle Slipover *page 43* Child's Fair Isle Yoked Sweater *page 47*
**Freya Hunter** Child's Fair Isle Cardigan with Beret *page 22* Chevron Lace Sweater *page 87* Shetland Lace Sweater with Cables *page 90*
**Fiona McTague** Fair Isle Sweater with Collar *page 19* Gansey Style Sweater *page 62* Lace and Cable Gansey *page 76* Child's Fair Isle Slipover *page 9* Family Aran Cardigans *page 112* Fisherman's Style Sweater *page 84*
**Gladys Amedro** Shetland Shoulder Shawl *page 16*
**Janet Macleod** Hebridean Gansey *page 96*
**Ina Irvine** Fair Isle V-Neck Cardigan with Beret *page 30* Vertical Fair Isle Cardigan *page 12*
**Laura Williamson** Man's Fair Isle Waistcoat *page 27* Fair Isle Sweater in Natural Shades *page 54*
**Kate Upcraft** Bobble Aran with Polo Neck *page 104* Lace and Cable Cardigan *page 93* Tree of Life Gansey *page 58* Aran Jacket with Lace Panels *page 80*

Knitting Photography: Sandra Lousada
Stylist: Marie Willey
Designer: Janet James
Island Photographs, pages 5, 6: The Still Moving Picture Company;
page 7: The Irish Tourist Board

Published by Crown Publishers Inc, 201 East 50th Street, New York, New York, 10022.
Member of Crown Publishing Group.

Originally published in Great Britain by Ebury Press in 1991.
Crown is a trademark of Crown Publishers, Inc.

Manufactured in Italy by New Interlitho, S.p.a., Milan.

Library of Congress Cataloging-in-Publication Data is available.

ISBN 0–517–58637–1

10  9  8  7  6  5  4  3  2  1

First American Edition

# CONTENTS

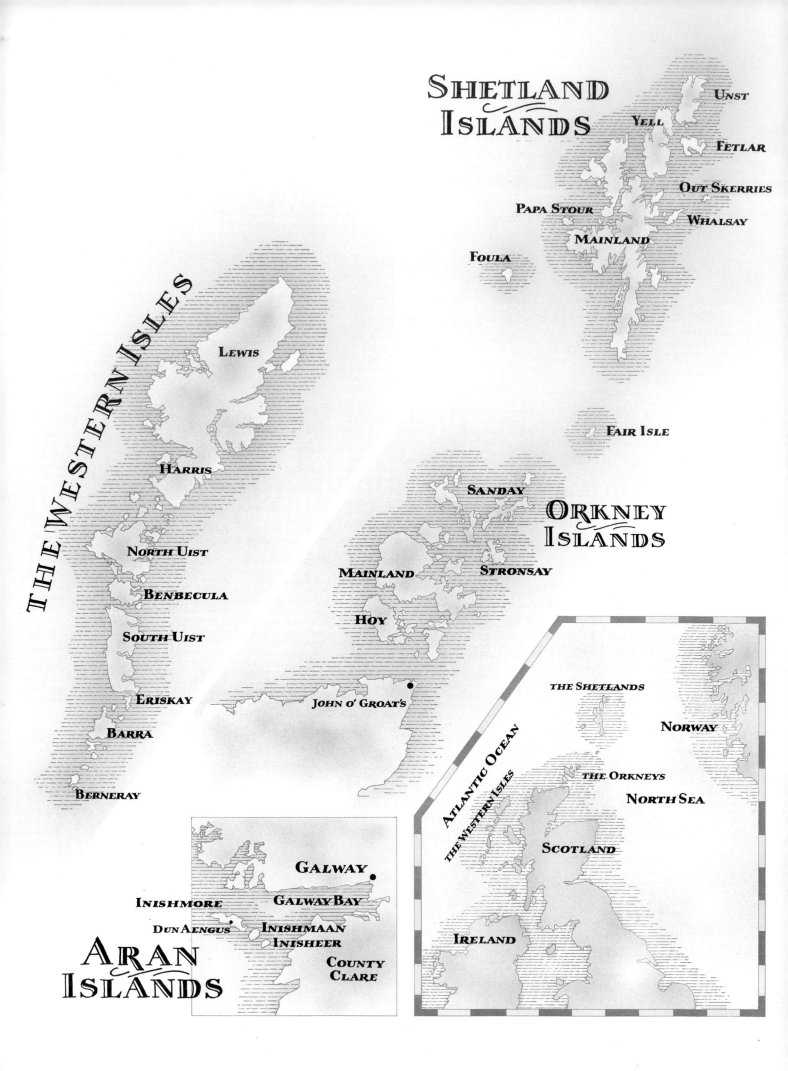

SHETLAND
ISLANDS

UNST

YELL

FETLAR

OUT SKERRIES

PAPA STOUR

WHALSAY

MAINLAND

FOULA

FAIR ISLE

THE WESTERN ISLES

LEWIS

HARRIS

SANDAY

ORKNEY
ISLANDS

NORTH UIST

BENBECULA

MAINLAND

STRONSAY

SOUTH UIST

HOY

ERISKAY

JOHN O' GROAT'S

BARRA

THE SHETLANDS

NORWAY

ATLANTIC OCEAN

THE WESTERN ISLES

THE ORKNEYS

NORTH SEA

BERNERAY

SCOTLAND

GALWAY

INISHMORE

GALWAY BAY

DUN AENGUS

INISHMAAN

IRELAND

INISHEER

ARAN
ISLANDS

COUNTY
CLARE

# THE ISLANDS

*T*he Shetland Islands make up the most northerly point of Britain. They are in fact closer to Norway than they are to mainland Scotland, and are made up of two main groups: the larger islands of Yell, Unst, Fetlar and Mainland; surrounded by the smaller islands of Out Skerries, Whalsay, Papa Stour, Foula and Fair Isle.

Although remote geographically, the islands have not been isolated, in that many sea routes converged on Shetland from the Baltic, Scandinavia, the North Sea and mainland Scotland. Traffic to the island began with the Vikings, and from 876 to 1379 Shetland was administered from Norway. Islanders today are justly proud of their Norse heritage.

Since the discovery of oil in the 1970s there have been many changes on Shetland. While oil has brought economic benefits, fishing is still of vital importance to the economy, and Shetland has contributed to the knitting boom with many new businesses, from the designer working on her own to large factories. It is difficult to know when knitting reached the islands but it seems to have appeared in Northern Europe and the Baltic around the sixteenth century.

The texture of the wool spun from Shetland sheep is soft, light and fine and is therefore more suitable for knitting than it is for weaving. Shetland wool was used to make exquisite lace shawls, fine enough to be pulled through a wedding ring.

This knitting was introduced to the London market, and in the 1840s there was a huge demand for lace mittens, veils and baby clothes; but by the end of the reign of Victoria machine-made lace was being manufactured in Nottingham, and handknitting could not compete.

Lace knitting is still popular in Shetland. Some young brides carry on the tradition of knitting their own wedding veils from patterns handed down through the generations the stitches taken from the land and seascape of the islands, and called Cockleshell, Print of the Wave, and Old Shell.

Fair Isle, which lies to the south of Shetland, has given its name to a unique form of knitting. The term Fair Isle has become a generic term to describe any kind of coloured knitting, but this is not strictly accurate as it is very specialized in design and colouring, differing even from work carried out within Shetland, by the use of more geometric patterning and richer shades.

It is almost impossible to trace the origins of this type of knitting, but there has been a link pointed out between it and the patterns found in the folk weaving of the Baltic and Russia. As Lerwick was a point of call for ships travelling between North America and the Baltic, this theory is now given much credence.

Fair Isle introduced the use of dyed wool for knitting before the days of chemical dyes, using

*Lerwick, Shetland*

*Carloway, Isle of Lewis*

a gold obtained from onions, an imported madder red, and indigo blue. These shades were traditionally used against a background of black, grey, fawn, brown and cream obtained from the natural shades of the sheep's wool.

Later on, chemical dyes were used but they often lacked the quality and richness of the natural dyes.

Fair Isle knitters worked in the round on sets of needles, working only in rows when dividing for the armholes, and knitting the sleeves down from the shoulders. Until the beginning of this century most Fair Isle in existence was in the form of small items such as caps, scarves and gloves, but from around 1900 all-over patterned garments started to appear.

Although much of the commercial work in the islands is now machine knitted, knitting is taught in every primary school in Shetland and learning to knit is as much part of growing up as learning to read and write. The tradition of handknitting is still very much alive, keeping the Fair Isle heritage alive and enriched.

In the mouth of the Galway Bay on the west coast of Ireland lie the islands of Aran. The islands were inhabited from the stone age and there is a wealth of pre-historic sites. Later came construction of the great stone forts for which the islands are famous, and of which Dun Aengus is the most well known.

Christianity came to Ireland in the early fifth century and with the later development of monasticism, monasteries and hermitages were built on the off-shore islands.

In the fourteenth century the O'Brien family of County Clare had an agreement with Galway to protect its shipping lanes from pirate attacks. In effect, in Elizabethan times Aran became the key point of the whole western coastal defence. It was not until the eighteenth century when strategy changed that Aran ceased to be of strategic importance and the islands passed into an existence of subsistence farming and fishing.

It is uncommon now to see the traditional dress of the Aran people, the full skirt of red or blue cloth, bawneen (Irish tweed) suits and pampooties, the raw hide shoes cut from untanned cowskin. The Aran sweater, however, with its patterns

passed down from generation to generation with-out any written instructions is now internationally famous, and the stitch patterns are an important component of any knitter's vocabulary.

Originally, of course, the sweaters were not worn as decorative items but as practical hardwearing garments to protect the wearer against the elements. Heavy patterning across the garment increased insulation, whilst the cabling, by crossing and twisting stitches, gave the fabric elasticity, allowing the wearer freedom of movement and comfort. The intricate patterns gave an almost three dimensional effect with the textures producing light and shadow, created by the placing of honeycombe next to cable and lattice with diamond.

The islander, knitting for her family, worked in her complex patterns creating individual sweaters without writing down the stitches, and passed on her knowledge from mother to daughter. Traditionally, patterns were kept within the family, more panels sometimes being added to celebrate a wedding or the birth of a baby. The backs were often different from the fronts, giving even more opportunity for a rich variety of patterning.

Many theories have been put forward in explanation of the origins of the unique patterns. One suggestion that the stitches had religious meaning; but the patterns could also symbolize the mesh of

*Great Magnus Bay, Shetland*

the fishermen's nets, the plaiting of their ropes and cables, and the stone walled fields of the islands.

There is still much to be learned about the history of Aran knitting, but whatever the source the Aran will always be one of the most beautiful and fascinating examples of the craft of handknitting.

The Hebrides form an archipelago of over 500 islands, many of them uninhabited, sweeping in a curve down the west coast of Scotland. The Outer Hebrides, known as The Western Isles, are the largest of the four main groups of islands, and consist of Lewis and Harris, and the smaller islands of Berneray, North Uist, Benbecula, South Uist, Barra and Eriskay. Many of the islands when approached from the mainland can look stark and forbidding, but on their western shores can be found sweeping beaches of shell-sand; and inland, there is a variety of landscapes from purple heathery moors to daisy-whitened fields.

Apart from crofting, the islands' main activity was fishing, which 100 years ago was in a boom period. Since then the Hebridean fishing industry has shrunk to a fraction of its former size, but at the turn of the century the herring ruled six days of every week in season. The fishermen sailed with their fleets on the trail of the herring around the coast of Scotland, working their way as far south as Norfolk. The women went too, to gut and pack the fish, and in the frequent lulls when few fish were being landed and in the evening, they would

*Aran Islands*

knit the traditional fisherman's guernsey or 'gansey' for the menfolk, exchanging stitch patterns by row chanting or committing the patterns to memory.

The fisherman's gansey, or 'fisherman's frock' was a practical garment knitted tightly on 5 ply worsted yarn to make it highly insulating. The yoke section, which covered the chest, was usually the most heavily patterned part to give the maximum protection against the elements, and because the garment fitted closely under-arm gussets were usually worked to allow for movement. Ganseys were knitted in the round, with the sleeve stitches picked up around the armholes and knitted down so that they could be more easily unravelled and re-knitted when worn out. Welts were often cast on and cuffs cast off with the yarn doubled to make them even more hard wearing, and while the body was fairly long and could be turned up when at work, the sleeves were shorter than normal to prevent them becoming wet and uncomfortable.

On this practical, virtually seamless garment, an endless variety of beautiful patterns were worked, all based on simple combinations of purl stitches; in diamonds, zig-zags and symbols of the fishing community such as anchors, worked against a plain background and sometimes framed with cables and moss stitch panels.

There is, however, one place where the patterns are virtually unique – in Eriskay, a tiny island between Barra and South Uist. Although crofting is the main activity of the islanders, they have also become first-class fishermen, and now they are attempting to make their unique Hebridean gansey contribute to the economy of the island. A co-operative was formed called Co Chomunn Erisgeidh Ltd which has revived the skill of knitting the Eriskay Jersey, and about a dozen women per year produce approximately fifty garments for the tourist trade. The yokes are distinctive in that the patterns, arranged in blocks, give a 'sampler' effect to the design.

Through projects like Co Chomunn Erisgeidh and the enthusiasm of knitters, the gansey tradition will remain alive, a lasting tribute to the fishing communities and their history.

# BASIC INFORMATION

## ABBREVIATIONS

alt-alternate, beg-begin(ning), cm-centimetres, cont-continue, dec-decreas(e)ing, foll-following, g-gramme, inc-increas(e)ing, in-inch(es), K-knit, m1-make one by picking up loop lying between st just worked and next st and work into the back of it, mm-millimetre, oz-ounce, patt-pattern, p-purl, psso-pass slipped stitch over, rem-remain(ing), rep-repeat, sl-slip, st st-stocking stitch, tbl-through back of loop(s), tog-together, yb-yarn back, yf-yarn forward, yon-yarn over needle, yrn-yarn round needle.

## NOTES

Figures for larger sizes are given in ( ) brackets. Where only one figure appears, this applies to all sizes.
Work figures given in [ ] the number of times stated afterwards. Where 0 appears no stitches or rows are worked for this size.

## YARNS

All amounts are based on average requirements and should therefore be regarded as approximate. Use only the yarn specified if at all possible; we cannot be responsible for an imperfect garment if any other brand is used.

## TENSION

Each pattern in this book specifies tension – the number of stitches and rows per centimetre (inch) that should be obtained on given needles, yarn and stitch pattern. Check your tension carefully before commencing work.

Use the same yarn, needles and stitch pattern as those to be used for main work and knit a sample at least 12.5×12.5 cm (5 in) square. Smooth out the finished sample on a flat surface but do not stretch it. To check the tension place a ruler horizontally on the sample and mark 10 cm (4 in) across with pins. Count the number of stitches between pins. To check the row tension place ruler vertically on sample and mark out 10 cm (4 in) with pins. Count the number of rows between pins. If the number of stitches and rows is greater than specified try again using larger needles; if less use smaller needles.

The stitch tension is the most important to get right.

## CIRCULAR KNITTING

Some of the garments in this book have been knitted in the round on circular or double pointed needles. Circular or tubular knitting is worked in continuous rounds to make a seamless fabric. A circular needle is used for large pieces and double pointed needles for smaller pieces, such as neckbands.

The approach to knitting is the same regardless of what method is used. There are a few important points to remember:

1 The bottom edge of all stitches must face the centre thus avoiding twisting the work.
2 A marker such as a length of coloured thread should be placed at the end of the cast on edge to indicate end of rounds, and moved up as the work progresses.
3 Yarn must be pulled firmly when knitting the first stitch of next round, or the first stitch on each of double pointed needles, to avoid a ladder effect.
4 Always read the chart from right to left.

**With a circular needle:** Cast on stitches in usual way. Join work by working into first cast on stitch, pulling yarn tightly to avoid a gap. Knit to marker, slip marker, begin the next round. When work is divided for back and front use a circular needle as straight needles.

**With a set of double pointed needles:** Divide the number of stitches to be picked up or cast on between three needles, leaving one needle free for working with. Lay the three needles in a triangle. With fourth (working) needle join work by working into first cast on stitch on first needle, pulling the yarn tightly to avoid a gap. Knit all stitches of first needle, and using this needle as a working needle, knit stitches of second and third needles as before. Slip marker and begin next round.

---

**FOR AMERICAN KNITTERS:** We strongly recommend using the yarns specified (following, in bold) for accurate, traditional results. If, however, these yarns are unobtainable, the following substitutions are best. Make sure that the tension is correct (see above), and that you buy equivalent weights of yarns. (* after specified yarn = available in US. See list of stockists below.)
**Jamieson and Smith Shetland 2-ply jumper weight\*:** Harrisville Designs Shetland style 2-ply, Rowan Botany, Brunswick Fairhaven fingering yarn. **Jamiesons Pure Shetland:** Harrisville Designs Shetland style 2-ply, Rowan Botany, Brunswick Fairhaven fingering yarn. **Wendy Guernsey 5-ply\*:** Tahki Sunbeam DK, Rowan Designer DK. **Jamieson and Smith Shetland 2-ply lace weight\*:** Harrisville Designs Harrisville Singles, Rowan Botany. **Wilkinson Guernsey 5 ply\*:** Wendy Guernsey 5ply, Tahki Sunbeam DK, Rowan Designer DK. **Hayfield Pure Wool Classic DK\*:** Tahki Sunbeam DK, Rowan Designer DK. **Hayfield Brig Aran:** Rowan Magpie, Tahki Sunbeam Aran, Brunswick Germantown, Tahki Donegal or Windsor Tweeds. **Cone of Cambrian Factory of Welsh Knitting Wool:** Harrisville Designs Harrisville 2-ply, Rowan Designer DK, Tahki Sunbeam DK. **Rowan Pure Wool DK\*:** Rowan Light DK.

## SPECIFIED YARN STOCKISTS

*The first four companies will supply yarn direct to the public. Please write for a price list enclosing a sae. Wilkinson Knitwear also produces a knitting kit for partially knitted traditional ganseys.*

**Wilkinson Knitwear,** 6, Tregavarras Row, Gorran, St Austell, Cornwall PL26 6LN. Tel: (0726) 843863. **Jamieson and Smith (Shetland Wool Brokers) Ltd,** 90 North Rd, Lerwick, Shetland ZE1 0BD. Tel: (0595) 3579. **Jamiesons Knitwear,** 93–95 Commercial Street, Lerwick, Shetland ZE1 0BD. Tel: (0595) 87285. **Welsh Knitting Wools,** The Cambrian Factory, Llanwrtyd, Powys, Wales LD5 4SD. Tel: (059) 13211. **Hayfield Textiles Limited,** Hayfield Mills, Glusburn, Keighley, W Yorkshire BD20 8QP. Tel: (0535) 633333. **Wendy Wools,** Carter and Parker Ltd, Gordon Mills, Guisley, W Yorkshire LS20 9PD. Tel: (0943) 872264. *For information regarding knitwear from Shetland contact:* **The Shetland Knitwear Trades, Association,** 175a Commercial Street, Lerwick, Shetland ZE1 0JL. Tel: (0595) 5631/5081. *For information regarding Co Chomunn Erisgeidh Ltd contact:* **Co Chomunn Erisgeidh Ltd,** Community Hall, Eriskay, South Uist, Tel: (08786) 236. *For information regarding Janet Macleod's knitwear contact:* **Janet Macleod Handknitwear,** 5 Churchill Drive, Stornaway, Isle of Lewis PA87 2NP.

## US YARN STOCKISTS

**Harrisville Designs,** Harrisville, NH 03450. Tel: (603) 8273333. **Rowan,** Westminster Trading Corp, 5 Northern Blvd, Amherst, NH 03031. Tel: (603) 8865041. **Brunswick Yarns,** Pickens, South Carolina 29671. Tel: (803) 8786375. **Tahki Sunbeam,** Tahki Imports Ltd, 11 Graphic Place, Moonachie, NJ 07074. Tel: (201) 8070070. **Wendy Wools,** Berroco, Elmdale Road, PO Box 367, Uxbridge, Mass 01569. Tel: (508) 2782527. **Hayfield,** Cascade, 204 Third Ave South, Seattle, Wash 98104. **Jamieson and Smith, and other wools used in this book,** The Wool Shop, 25 The Plaza, Locust Valley, NY 11560. Tel: (516) 6719722.

## AUSTRALIAN YARN STOCKISTS

**Hayfield,** Panda Yarns Ltd, 314–320 Albert Street, Brunswick, VIC 3057. **Wendy Wools,** TCW Pty Ltd, 30 Guess Avenue, Arncliffe, NSW 2205.

## MATERIALS

2×2oz hanks of Jamieson and Smith Shetland 2 ply Jumper Weight in Grey (2) M.
1×2oz hank of same in each of Brown (4) and Cream (1a).
1x1oz hank of same in each of Red (125), Blue (142), Green (34) and Mustard (121).
1 pair in each of 2¾mm (No 12/US 2) and 3¼ mm (No 10/US 4) knitting needles.

## MEASUREMENTS

To fit chest 56(61:66)cm
22(24:26)in
All round at chest 64(70:76)cm
25¼(27½:30)in
Length to shoulder 35(39:42)cm
13¾(15½:16½)in

## TENSION

29 sts and 29 rows to 10cm/4in square measured over patt on 3¼mm (No 10/US 4) needles.

## ABBREVIATIONS

See page 8.

## NOTE

When working patt from chart, read K rows from right to left and P rows from left to right.
Strand yarn not in use loosely across wrong side to keep fabric elastic.

# CHILD'S FAIR ISLE SLIPOVER

❖

### FRONT

With 2¾mm (No 12/US 2) needles and M, cast on 79(85:91) sts.
**1st row (right side)** K1, [P1, K1] to end.
**2nd row** P1, [K1, P1] to end.
Rep these 2 rows until welt measures 6cm/2¼in from beg, ending with a right side row.
**Next row** Rib 6(4:2), [inc in next st, rib 4] to last 8(6:4) sts, inc in next st, rib 7(5:3). 93(101:109) sts.
Change to 3¼mm (No 10/US 4) needles.
Beg with a K row, work in st st and patt from chart until work measures 21(24:26)cm/8¼(9½: 10¼)in from beg, ending with a wrong side row. ★★

### Shape Armhole and Neck

**Next row** Cast off 4, patt until there are 40(44:48) sts on right-hand needle, K2 tog, turn. Work on this set of sts only.
Keeping patt correct, dec one st at each end of 6 foll right side rows. 29(33:37) sts. Keeping armhole edge straight, cont dec one st at neck edge on every right side row until 19(21:23) sts rem.
Cont without shaping until work measures 35(39:42)cm/13¾(15½:16½)in from beg, ending with a wrong side row. Cast off.
With right side facing, slip centre one st onto a safety pin, rejoin yarn to rem 46(50:54) sts, K2 tog, patt to end. Cast off 4 sts at beg of next row. Complete to match first side.

### BACK

Work as given for Front to ★★.

### Shape Armholes

Cast off 4 sts at beg of next 2 rows. Dec one st at each end of next and 5 foll alt rows. 73(81:89) sts.
Cont without shaping until work measures same as Front to cast off edge, ending with a wrong side row.

### Shape Shoulders

**Next row** Cast off 19(21:23) sts, patt to last 19(21:23) sts, cast off these sts. Leave rem 35(39:43) sts on a holder.

## NECKBAND

Join right shoulder seam.
With 2¾mm (No 12/US 2) needles, M and right side facing, pick up and K 42(46:48) sts down left front neck, K centre front st from safety pin, pick up and K 42(46:48) sts up right front neck, K back neck sts dec 4 sts evenly. 116(128:136) sts.
**1st row** K1, [P1, K1] to within 2 sts of centre front st, P2 tog, P1, P2 tog tbl, [K1, P1] to end.
**2nd row** K1, [P1, K1] to within 2 sts of centre front st, K2 tog tbl, K1, K2 tog, [K1, P1] to end.
Rep these 2 rows 4 times more. Cast off in rib dec as before.

## ARMBANDS

Join left shoulder and neckband seam.
With 2¾mm (No 12/US 2) needles, M and right side facing, pick up and K 92(96:100) sts evenly around armhole edge.
Work 10 rows in K1, P1 rib. Cast off in rib.

## TO MAKE UP

Pin piece out to correct measurements and press with a warm iron over a damp cloth.
Join side and armband seams. Press seams.

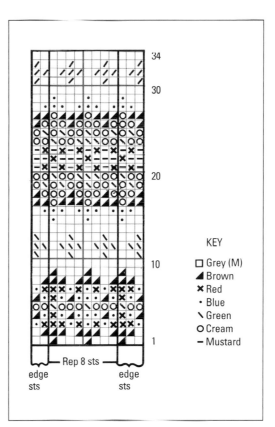

KEY
□ Grey (M)
◢ Brown
✕ Red
• Blue
╲ Green
○ Cream
− Mustard

— Rep 8 sts —
edge sts          edge sts

## MATERIALS

2(2:2:3) 2oz hanks of Jamieson and Smith Shetland 2 ply Jumper Weight in Cream (1a) A.
2×2oz hanks of same in Shetland Black (5) C.
3×1oz hanks of same in Mustard (28) D.
4(4:5:5) 1oz hanks of Jamiesons Pure Shetland in Blue (726) B.
2(2:2:3) 1oz hanks of same in Red (577) E.
One in each of 2¼mm (No 13/US 2) and 3mm (No 11/US 4) circular needles.
One set of four in each of 2¼mm (No 13/US 2) and 3mm (No 11/US 4) double pointed knitting needles.
1 pair in each of 2¼mm (No 13/US 2) and 3mm (No 11/US 4) knitting needles.
7 buttons.

## MEASUREMENTS

To fit bust
81-87(91-97:102-107:112-117)cm
32-34(36-38:40-42:44-46)in
All round at bust 104(110:122:127)cm
41(43¼:48:50)in
Length to shoulder 61(62:63:64)cm
24(24½:24¾:25¼)in
Sleeve length 52cm/20½in

## TENSION

30 sts and 30 rows to 10cm/4in square measured over patt on 3mm (No 11/US 4) needles.

## ABBREVIATIONS

See page 8.

## NOTE

When working in patt from chart, read K rounds or rows from right to left and P rows from left to right.
Strand yarn not in use loosely across wrong side to keep fabric elastic.

# VERTICAL FAIR ISLE CARDIGAN

### POCKET LININGS
MAKE 2

With 3mm (No 11/US 4) needles and B, cast on 37 sts. Beg with a K row and working in st st throughout, work patt from chart as follows:
**1st row** Work last 6 sts of 1st row of chart, then rep 26 sts once, work first 5 sts.
**2nd row** Work last 5 sts of 2nd row of chart, then rep 26 sts once, work first 6 sts.
These 2 rows set patt. Cont working in patt from chart as set until 31st row of chart has been worked. Leave these sts on a holder.

### MAIN PART
WORKED IN ONE PIECE TO ARMHOLES

With 2¼mm (No 13/US 2) circular needle and B, cast on 246(258:290:306) sts. Work backwards and forwards in rib as follows:
**1st row (wrong side)** P2, [K2, P2] to end.
**2nd row** K2C, [B yarn forward, P2B, B yarn back, K2C] to end.
**3rd row** P2C, [B yarn back, K2B, B yarn forward, P2C] to end.
**4th and 5th rows** As 2nd and 3rd rows.
**6th to 9th rows** As 2nd to 5th rows, but using E instead of C.
**10th to 13th rows** As 2nd to 5th rows, but using D instead of C.
**14th to 17th rows** As 6th to 9th rows.
**18th to 21st rows** As 2nd to 5th rows.
**Next row** With B, K2(2:6:6), ★[inc in next st, K3] 7(10:6:4) times, inc in next st, K7; rep from ★ to last 28(16:28:12) sts, [inc in next st, K3] 7(4:7:3) times. 301(317:353:369) sts.
Change to 3mm (No 11/US 4) circular needle. P 1 row in B.
Beg with a K row and working in st st throughout, work in patt from chart as follows:
**1st row (right side)** Work last 8(3:8:3) sts of 1st row of chart, then rep 26 sts 11(12:13:14) times, work first 7(2:7:2) sts.
**2nd row** Work last 7(2:7:2) sts of 2nd row of chart, then rep 26 sts 11(12:13:14) times, work first 8(3:8:3) sts.
These 2 rows set patt. Cont in patt as set until 31st row of chart has been worked.

### Place Pocket

**Next row** Patt 28(23:28:23), sl next 37 sts onto a holder, patt across sts of first pocket lining, patt to last 65(60:65:60) sts, slip next 37 sts onto a holder, patt across sts of second pocket lining, patt to end.

Cont in patt across all sts until work measures 35(36:37:38)cm/13¾(14:14½:15)in from beg, ending with a wrong side row.

### Shape Fronts

**Next row** Patt 2, K2 tog tbl, patt to last 4 sts, K2 tog, patt 2.
**Next 2 rows** Patt to end.
**Next row** Patt 2, P2 tog, patt to last 4 sts, P2 tog tbl, patt 2.
**Next 2 rows** Patt to end.
Rep last 6 rows once more. 293(309:345:361) sts.

### Divide work as follows

**Next row** Patt 2, K2 tog tbl, patt 54(62:67:75), turn.
Work on this set of sts only for Right Front.
**Next row** Patt to end.
**Next row** Patt 2, K2 tog tbl, patt to last 3 sts, K2 tog, patt 1.
Rep last 2 rows 6 times more. 43(51:56:64) sts.
**1st and 3rd sizes only**
**Next 3 rows** Patt to end.
**Next row** Patt 2, K2 tog tbl, patt to end.
Rep last 4 rows until 32(43) sts rem.
**2nd and 4th sizes only**
**Next row** Patt to end.
**Next row** Patt 2, K2 tog tbl, patt to end.
Rep last 2 rows (4:11) times more.
**Next 2 rows** Patt to end.
**Next row** Patt to last 4 sts, p2 tog tbl, patt 2.
**Next 2 rows** Patt to end.
**Next row** Patt 2, K2 tog tbl, patt to end.
Rep last 6 rows until (32:43) sts rem.
**All sizes**
Cont without shaping until work measures 61(62:63:64)cm/24(24½:24¾:25¼)in from beg, ending with a wrong side row dec one st at end of last row. Leave these sts on a spare needle.
With right side facing, slip next 21 sts onto a holder, rejoin yarn to rem sts and patt 135(135:161:161) sts, turn. Work on this set of sts only for Back.
**Next row** Patt to end.
**Next row** Patt 1, K2 tog tbl, patt to last 3 sts, K2 tog, patt 1.

Rep last 2 rows 6 times more. 121(121:147:147) sts.

Cont without shaping until work measures same as Right Front, ending with a wrong side row. Leave these sts on a spare needle.

With right side facing, slip next 21 sts onto a holder, rejoin yarn to rem sts for Left Front and patt to last 4 sts, K2 tog, patt 2.
**Next row** Patt to end.
**Next row** Patt 1, K2 tog tbl, patt to last 4 sts, K2 tog, patt 2.
Rep last 2 rows 6 times more. 43(51:56:64) sts.
**1st and 3rd sizes only**
**Next 3 rows** Patt to end.
**Next row** Patt to last 4 sts, K2 tog, patt 2.
Rep last 4 rows until 32(43) sts rem.
**2nd and 4th sizes only**
**Next row** Patt to end.
**Next row** Patt to last 4 sts, K2 tog, patt 2.
Rep last 2 rows (4:11) times more.
**Next 2 rows** Patt to end.
**Next row** Patt 2, P2 tog, patt to end.
**Next 2 rows** Patt to end.
**Next row** Patt to last 4 sts, K2 tog, patt 2.
Rep last 6 rows until (32:43) sts rem.
**All sizes**
Cont without shaping until work measures same as Back, ending with a wrong side row dec one st at beg of last row.

### Join Shoulders

With right sides of Back and Fronts together, cast off together 31(31:42:42) shoulder sts (see diagram page 39), leaving centre 59(59:63:63) back neck sts on a holder.

### SLEEVES

With set of four 3mm (No 11/US 4) needles, B and right side facing, slip first 11 sts from holder at one armhole edge onto a safety pin, join in yarn and K rem 10 sts, pick up and K 109 sts evenly around armhole edge, K11 sts from safety pin. 130 sts.

Mark end of last round to denote end of rounds. Work in rounds of st st (every round K) and patt from chart as follows:
**1st round** Work last 13(0:0:13) sts of 61st row of chart, rep 26 sts 4(5:5:4) times, work first 13(0:0:13) sts.
This round sets patt. Cont in patt to match Back working rows of chart in reverse order, **at the same time**, dec one st at each end of 32nd round, then on every foll 5th round until 90 sts

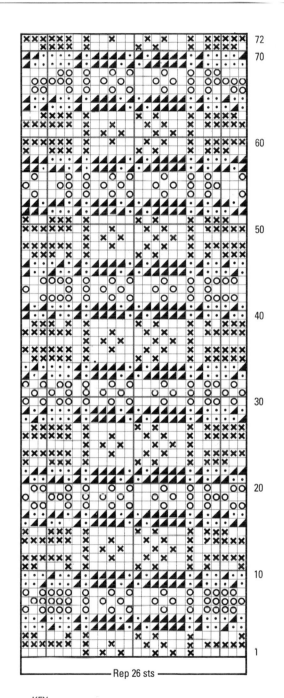

— Rep 26 sts —

**KEY**

☐ Cream (A)
✕ Blue (B)
• Shetland Black (C)
◢ Mustard (D)
○ Red (E)

rem. Patt 5 rounds. With B, work 1 round.
**Next round** With B, [K1, K2 tog] to end. 60 sts.
Change to set of four 2¼mm (No 13/US 2) needles.
**1st to 4th rounds** [P2B, B yarn back, K2C, B yarn forward] to end.
**5th to 8th rounds** As 1st to 4th rounds, but using E instead of C.
**9th to 12th rounds** As 1st to 4th rounds, but using D instead of C.
**13th to 16th rounds** As 5th to 8th rounds.
**17th to 20th rounds** As 1st to 4th rounds.
With B, rib 1 round. Cast off in rib.

### FRONT BAND

With 2¼mm (No 13/US 2) circular needle, B, right side facing and working between 2nd and 3rd st, pick up and K 104(106:108:110) sts evenly along straight edge of Right Front, K80 sts along shaped edge to shoulder, K across 59(59:63:63) back neck sts dec 5 sts evenly, pick up and K80 sts evenly along shaped edge of Left Front and 104(106:108:110) sts along straight edge.
422(426:434:438) sts.
Work backwards and forwards in rib as follows:
**1st row** P2D, [B yarn back, K2B, B yarn forward, P2D] to end.
**2nd row** K2D, [B yarn forward, P2B, B yarn back, K2D] to end.
Rep these 2 rows once more.
**1st buttonhole row** Using E instead of D rib as 1st row making buttonholes as follows: rib

to last 104 sts, [cast off 2, rib 14 including st used in casting off] 6 times, cast off 2, rib to end.
**2nd buttonhole row** Using E instead of D, rib as 2nd row casting on 2 sts over those cast off in previous row.
**Next row** As 1st row, but using E instead of D.
**Next row** As 2nd row, but using E instead of D.
**Next row** As 1st row, but using C instead of D.
**Next row** As 2nd row, but using C instead of D.
Rep last 2 rows once more. With B, rib 1 row. Cast off in rib.

### POCKET TOPS

With 2¼mm (No 13/US 2) needles, B and right side facing, K across sts of one pocket top dec 3 sts evenly. 34 sts.
Now work 3rd to 5th rows, then work 2nd row of rib patt as given for Main Part. With B, rib 1 row. Cast off in rib.

### TO COMPLETE

With 2¼mm (No 13/US 2) needles, B and right side facing, pick up and K 13 sts along row ends of front band. Cast off. Work other side in same way.
Catch down pocket linings and sides of pocket tops. Fold back the 2 stitch edge on wrong side of fronts and neatly stitch in place.
Hand wash in lukewarm water. Pat dry in towel. Stretch out to size and shape and dry flat away from heat and sunlight. Sew on buttons when dry.

# SHETLAND SHOULDER SHAWL

## MATERIALS

4×1oz hanks of Jamieson and Smith
Shetland 2 ply Lace Weight.
1 pair of 4½mm (No 7/US 6) knitting
needles.
One 4½mm (No 7/US 6) circular
needle, 80cm long.

## MEASUREMENTS

Approximately 114×114×172cm
45×45×68in measured diagonally.

## ABBREVIATIONS

Pw-purlwise
Also see page 8.

## EDGING

With 4½mm (No 7/US 6) needles cast on 11 sts very loosely. K 1 row.

**1st row** Sl 1Pw, K2 tog, yf, K2 tog, K6. 10 sts.
**2nd and every alt row (right side)** Sl 1Pw, K to end.
**3rd row** Sl 1 Pw, K1, yf, K2 tog, yf, K6. 11 sts.
**5th row** Sl 1Pw, K1, [yf, K2 tog] twice, yf, K5. 12 sts.
**7th row** Sl 1Pw, K1, [yf, K2 tog] 3 times, yf, K4. 13 sts.
**9th row** Sl 1Pw, K1, [yf, K2 tog] 4 times, yf, K3. 14 sts.
**11th row** Sl 1Pw, K2 tog, [yf, K2 tog] 4 times, K3. 13 sts.
**13th row** Sl 1Pw, K2 tog, [yf, K2 tog] 3 times, K4. 12 sts.
**15th row** Sl 1Pw, K2 tog, [yf, K2 tog] twice, K5. 11 sts.
**16th row** Sl 1Pw, K to end.
These 16 rows form patt. Rep these 16 rows 42 times more, then work 1st and 2nd rows again. K 1 row. Leave these sts on a safety pin.

## MAIN PART

With 4½mm (No 7/US 6) circular needle and right side facing, pick up and K tbl 344 sts along long, straight edge of edging. K 1 row.
**Next row** K1, [yf, K2 tog] to last st, K1.
K 2 rows. P 1 row. K 1 row.
**Next row** K12 and sl these sts onto a safety pin, K to last 12 sts, sl last 12 sts onto a safety pin, turn. 320 sts.
Work in patt across centre sts as follows:
**1st row (right side)** K1, [K2 tog] twice, * [yf, K1] 5 times, yf, [K2 tog] 3 times, K1, [K2 tog] 3 times *; rep from * to * 7 times more, [yf, K1] 5 times, yf, K1, K2 tog, K3 tog tbl, K1 (mark this st), K3 tog, K2 tog, K1; rep from * to * 8 times, [yf, K1] 5 times, yf, K2 tog tbl, K2. 323 sts.
**2nd row** K.
**3rd row** K1, K2 tog, K to 2 sts before marked st, K2 tog tbl, K1, K2 tog, K to last 3 sts, K2 tog tbl, K1.
**4th row** P.
**5th row** As 3rd row.
**6th row** K.
**7th row** K1, [K2 tog] twice, [yf, K1] 4 times, yf, * [K2 tog] 3 times, K1, [K2 tog] 3 times, [yf, K1] 5 times, yf *; rep from * to * 6 times more, [K2 tog] 3 times, K1, [K2 tog] 3 times,

[yf, K1] 5 times, K2 tog, K2 tog tbl, K1, [K2 tog] twice, [K1, yf] 5 times, rep from * to * 7 times, [K2 tog] 3 times, K1, [K2 tog] 3 times, yf, [K1, yf] 4 times, K2 tog, K2 tog tbl, K1. 315 sts.
**8th to 12th rows** Work 2nd to 6th rows. 307 sts.
**13th row** K1, [K2 tog] twice, [yf, K1] twice, yf, [K2 tog] 3 times, K1, [K2 tog] 3 times, * [yf, K1] 5 times, yf, [K2 tog] 3 times, K1, [K2 tog] 3 times *; rep from * to * 6 times more, [yf, K1] 3 times, yf, K2 tog, K2 tog tbl, K1, [K2

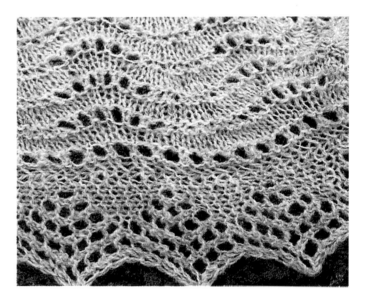

tog] twice, [yf, K1] 3 times, yf, [K2 tog] 3 times, K1, [K2 tog] 3 times, rep from * to * 7 times, yf, [K1, yf] twice, K2 tog, K2 tog tbl, K1. 301 sts.
**14th to 18th rows** Work 2nd to 6th rows. 293 sts.
**19th row** K1, K2 tog, ** [yf, K1] twice, yf, [K2 tog] twice, K1, * [K2 tog] 3 times, [yf, K1] 5 times, yf, [K2 tog] 3 times, K1*; rep from * to * 6 times more, [K2 tog] twice, [yf, K1] twice, yf **; K2 tog, K2 tog tbl, K1, [K2 tog] twice, rep from ** to ** once, K2 tog tbl, K1. 291 sts.
**20th to 24th rows** Work as 2nd to 6th rows. 283 sts.
**25th row** K1, K2 tog, K1, ** yf, K1, yf, K2 tog, K1, * [K2 tog] 3 times, [yf, K1] 5 times, yf, [K2 tog] 3 times, K1*; rep from * to * 6 times more, K2 tog, yf, K1, yf **; K2 tog, K2 tog tbl, K1, [K2 tog] twice, rep from ** to **

once, K1, K2 tog tbl, K1. 281 sts.

**26th to 30th rows** Work 2nd to 6th rows. 273 sts.

**31st row** K1, ** [K2 tog] twice, yf, K1, * [K2 tog] 3 times, [yf, K1] 5 times, yf, [K2 tog] 3 times, K1 *; rep from * to * to 4 sts before marked st (last st on next rep), yf, K2 tog, K2 tog tbl, K1 **; rep from ** to ** once.

**32nd to 36th rows** Work 2nd to 6th rows.

**37th row** K1, ** [K2 tog] 4 times, * [yf, K1] 5 times, yf, [K2 tog] 3 times, K1, [K2 tog] 3 times *; rep from * to * to 13 sts before marked st, [yf, K1] 5 times, yf, [K2 tog] 3 times, K2 tog tbl, K1 **; rep from ** to ** once.

**38th to 42nd rows** Work 2nd to 6th rows.

**43rd row** K1, ** [K2 tog] 3 times, [yf, K1] 4 times, yf, * [K2 tog] 3 times, K1, [K2 tog] 3 times, [yf, K1] 5 times, yf *; rep from * to * to 23 sts before marked st, [K2 tog] 3 times, K1, [K2 tog] 3 times, [yf, K1] 4 times, yf, [K2 tog] twice, K2 tog tbl, K1 **; rep from ** to ** once.

**44th to 48th rows** Work 2nd to 6th rows.

**49th row** K1, ** [K2 tog] twice, [yf, K1] 3 times, yf, [K2 tog] 3 times, K1, [K2 tog] 3 times, * [yf, K1] 5 times, yf, [K2 tog] 3 times, K1, [K2 tog] 3 times *; rep from * to * to 7 sts before marked st, [yf, K1] 3 times, yf, K2 tog, K2 tog tbl, K1 **; rep from ** to ** once.

**50th to 54th rows** Work 2nd to 6th rows.

**55th row** K1, ** [K2 tog] twice, [yf, K1] twice, yf, [K2 tog] twice, K1, * [K2 tog] 3 times, [yf, K1] 5 times, yf, [K2 tog] 3 times, K1 *; rep from * to * to 10 sts before marked st, [K2 tog] twice, [yf, K1] twice, yf, K2 tog, K2 tog tbl, K1 **; rep from ** to ** once.

**56th to 60th rows** Work 2nd to 6th rows.

**61st row** K1, ** [K2 tog] twice, yf, K1, yf, K2 tog, K1, * [K2 tog] 3 times, [yf, K1] 5 times, yf, [K2 tog] 3 times, K1 *; rep from * to * to 7 sts before marked st, K2 tog, yf, K1, yf, K2 tog, K2 tog tbl, K1 **; rep from ** to ** once.

**62nd to 66th rows** Work 2nd to 6th rows. 201 sts.

Rep 31st to 66th rows once (129 sts), then work 31st to 42nd rows again (105 sts).

Now work 43rd to 66th rows (57 sts), then work 31st to 36th rows again omitting rep from * to * (45 sts).

**Next row** K1, * [K2 tog] 4 times, [yf, K1] 5 times, yf, [K2 tog] 3 times, K2 tog tbl, K1 *;

rep from * to * once.

**Next row** K.

**Next row** K1, * K2 tog, K15, K2 tog tbl, K1 *; rep from * to * once. 37 sts. P 1 row. Break off yarn.

With right side facing, rejoin yarn at inside edge of the 12 sts left on a safety pin at right-hand side, pick up and K 147 sts along right side edge to centre 37 sts, K16, K2 tog tbl, K1, K2 tog, K16, pick up and K 146 sts along left side edge then pick up 1 st and K this st tog with 1st st on a safety pin, turn. 329 sts.

**Next row** K to last st, K last st tog with 1st st on a safety pin, turn.

Work in patt as follows:

**1st row** K2, [yf, K2 tog] to centre st, yf, K1, yf, [K2 tog, yf] to last 2 sts, K1, K last st tog with next st on a safety pin, turn. 331 sts.

**2nd and 3rd rows** K to last st, K last st tog with next st on a safety pin, turn.

**4th row** P to last st, P last st tog with next st on a safety pin, turn.

**5th and 6th rows** As 2nd and 3rd rows.

**7th row** [K2 tog] 5 times, * [yf, K1] 5 times, yf, [K2 tog] 3 times, K1, [K2 tog] 3 times; rep from * to last 15 sts, [yf, K1] 5 times, yf, [K2 tog] 4 times, K last 2 sts tog with next st on safety pin, turn. 327 sts.

**8th to 12th rows** Work 2nd to 6th rows.

**13th row** [K2 tog] 4 times, * [yf, K1] 5 times, yf, [K2 tog] 3 times, K1, [K2 tog] 3 times; rep from * to last 13 sts, [yf, K1] 5 times, yf, [K2 tog] 3 times, K last 2 sts tog with next st on a safety pin, turn. 325 sts.

**14th to 18th rows** Work 2nd to 6th rows.

**19th row** * K1, [K2 tog] 3 times, [yf, K1] 5 times, yf, [K2 tog] 3 times; rep from * to last st, K last st tog with next st on a safety pin, turn.

**20th and 21st rows** As 2nd and 3rd rows.

**22nd row** P to last st, P last st tog with last st on a safety pin, then pick up and P 5 and K 10 sts across edging.

Cast off knitwise, picking up and casting off 15 sts across other end of edging.

### TO COMPLETE

Hand wash in lukewarm water. Pat dry in towel. Stretch out to size and shape, pinning points of edging. Dry flat away from heat or sunlight.

## MATERIALS

3×2oz hanks of Jamieson and Smith
Shetland 2 ply Jumper Weight in Grey
(2) M.
2×2oz hanks of same in Cream (1a) A.
2×1oz hanks of same in each of Red
(93), Sunshine Yellow (91), Light
Yellow (66) and Green (34).
1×2oz hank of same in Mid Brown (4).
1×1oz hank of same in each of Light
Brown (61), Rust (125) and Blue (15).
1 pair in each of 2¾mm (No 12/US 2)
and 3¼ mm (No 10/US 4) knitting
needles.
One 2¾mm (No 12/US 2) circular
needle, 40cm long.

## MEASUREMENTS

To fit bust 86(91:97)cm
34(36:38)in
All round at bust 120(126:131)cm
47¼(49½:51½)in
Length to shoulder 56(58:60)cm
22(22¾:23½)in
Sleeve seam 49(50:51)cm
19¼(19¾:20)in

## TENSION

29 sts and 29 rows to 10cm/4in square
measured over patt on 3¼mm (No 10/
US 4) needles.

## ABBREVIATIONS

See page 8.

## NOTE

When working patt from chart, read K
rows from right to left and P rows from
left to right.
Strand yarn not in use loosely across
wrong side to keep fabric elastic.

# FAIR ISLE
# SWEATER
# WITH
# COLLAR

---◆◇◆---

### BACK

With 2¾mm (No 12/US 2) needles and M, cast
on 132(138:144) sts. Work in K1, P1 rib for
8cm/3in.
**Next row** Rib 2, [inc in next st, rib 2] to last 1
st, rib 1. 175(183:191) sts.
Change to 3¼mm (No 10/US 4) needles.
Beg with a K row, work in st st and patt from
chart until work measures 32(33:35)cm/12½(13:
13¾)in from beg, ending with a wrong side
row.

### Shape Armholes

Keeping patt correct, cast off 6 sts at beg of
next 2 rows. Dec one st at each end of next and
every foll alt row until 151(159:167) sts rem.★★
Cont without shaping until work measures
56(58:60)cm/22(22¾:23½)in from beg, ending
with a wrong side row.

### Shape Shoulders

Cast off 24(26:27) sts at beg of next 2 rows and
24(25:27) sts at beg of foll 2 rows. Leave rem
55(57:59) sts on a holder.

### FRONT

Work as given for Back to ★★. Cont without
shaping until work measures 48(50:52)cm/
19(19¾:20½)in from beg, ending with a wrong
side row.

### Shape Neck

**Next row** Patt 62(65:68), turn. Work on this
set of sts only.
Keeping patt correct, dec one st at neck edge
on next 10 rows, then on every alt row until
48(51:54) sts rem.
Cont without shaping until work measures
same as Back to shoulder shaping, ending at
armhole edge.

### Shape Shoulder

Cast off 24(26:27) sts at beg of next row. Work
1 row. Cast off rem 24(25:27) sts.
With right side facing, slip centre 27(29:31) sts
onto a holder, rejoin yarn to rem sts and patt
to end. Complete to match first side.

## SLEEVES

With 2¾mm (No 12/US 2) needles and M, cast on 66(68:70) sts. Work in K1, P1 rib for 8cm/3in.

**Next row** Rib 2(1:4), [inc in next st, rib 2(1:1), inc in next st, rib 2] to last 4(2:6) sts, inc in next st, rib 3(1:5). 87(95:95) sts.

Change to 3¼mm (No 10/US 4) needles.

Beg with a K row, work in st st and patt from chart as indicated for 2nd(1st:1st) size on Back, **at the same time**, inc one st at each end of 5th and 9(5:5) foll 3rd rows, then on every foll 4th row until there are 141(147:147) sts, working inc sts into patt.

Cont without shaping until work measures 49(50:51)cm/19¼(19¾:20)in from beg, ending with a wrong side row.

### Shape Top

Keeping patt correct, cast off 6 sts at beg of next 2 rows, 5 sts at beg of foll 4 rows and 7 sts at beg of foll 6 rows. Patt 2 rows. Cast off rem 67(73:73) sts.

## COLLAR

Join shoulder seams.

With 2¾mm (No 12/US 2) circular needle and right side facing, slip first 14(15:16) sts on front neck holder onto a safety pin, rejoin M yarn and K rem 13(14:15) sts, pick up and K 27 sts up right front neck, K across 55(57:59) back neck sts, pick up and K 27 sts down left front neck, then K 14(15:16) sts from safety pin. 136(140:144) sts. Work in rounds of K1, P1 rib for 2cm/¾in, dec one st at end of last round, turn. Now work backwards and forwards as follows:

**Next row** Rib 3, work 3 times in next st, rib to last 4 sts, work 3 times in next st, rib 3.

Rib 1 row. Rep last 2 rows until work measures 10cm/4in from beg. Cast off loosely in rib.

## TO MAKE UP

Pin pieces out to correct measurements and press with a warm iron over a damp cloth. Join side and sleeve seams. Sew in sleeves. Press seams.

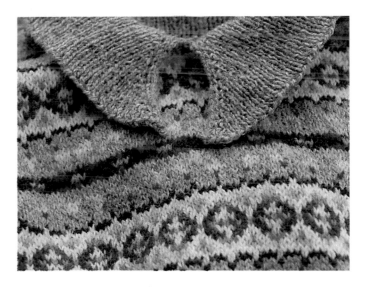

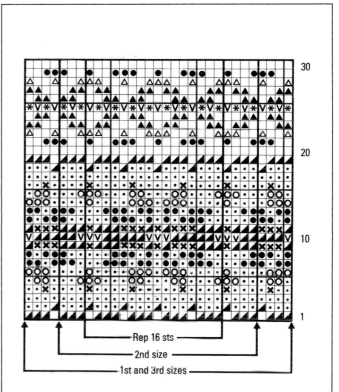

KEY

| | |
|---|---|
| □ Cream (M) | ● Sunshine Yellow |
| • Grey (A) | V Blue |
| ◢ Green | △ Light Brown |
| ✘ Red | ▲ Mid Brown |
| O Light Yellow | ✳ Rust |

## MATERIALS

*Cardigan* 4(4:5) 1oz hanks of Jamiesons
Pure Shetland in Red (500) M.
4(4:5) 1oz hanks of same in Mid Blue
(170) A.
1×2oz hank of same in White (304) B.
1(1:2) 1oz hanks of same in each of
Yellow (350) C and Royal Blue (665) D.
*Beret* 1×1oz hank of Jamiesons Pure
Shetland in each of Red (500) M and
Mid Blue (170) A.
Small amounts of same in each of White
(304) B, Yellow (350) C and Royal Blue
(665) D.
One in each of 2mm (No 14/US 2)
and 2¼mm (No 13/US 4) circular
needles.
One set of four in each of 2mm (No 14/
US 2) and 2¼mm (No 13/US 4)
double pointed knitting needles.
One pair of 2mm (No 14/US 2)
knitting needles.
7 buttons.

## MEASUREMENTS

To fit chest 61(66:71)cm/24(26:28)in
All round at chest 68(76:83)cm
26¾(30:32½)in
Length to shoulder 38(41:44)cm
15(16:17¼)in
Sleeve length 30(33:36)cm
11¾(13:14)in

## TENSION

33 sts and 35 rows to 10cm/4in square
measured over patt on 2¼mm (No 13/
US 4) needles.

## ABBREVIATIONS

See page 8.

## NOTE

When working in patt from chart, read
K rounds or rows from right to left and
P rows from left to right.
Strand yarn not in use loosely across
wrong side to keep fabric elastic.

# CHILD'S FAIR ISLE CARDIGAN WITH BERET

--❖--

## *CARDIGAN*

### MAIN PART

With 2mm (No 14/US 2) circular needle and
M, cast on 206(230:250) sts. Work backwards
and forwards as follows:
**1st row (right side)** K2, [P2, K2] to end.
**2nd row** P2, [K2, P2] to end.
**3rd row** K2C, [M yarn forward, P2M, M yarn
back, K2C] to end.
**4th row** P2C, [M yarn back, K2M, M yarn
forward, P2C] to end.
**5th to 8th rows**: Rep 3rd to 4th rows twice.
**9th to 14th rows** Work 3rd to 8th rows, but
using B instead of C.
**15th to 20th rows** Work 3rd to 8th rows.
**Next row** With M, K6(6:10), [K twice in next
st, K15(19:11), K twice in next st, K15] to last
8(8:16) sts, K twice in next st, K to end.
219(243:267) sts.
Change to 2¼mm (No 13/US 4) circular
needle.
Beg with a P row and working in st st throughout, work 2 rows.
Now work in patt from chart until work
measures 22(24:26)cm/8¾(9½:10¼)in from
beg, ending with a wrong side row.

### *Divide work as follows*
**Next row** Patt 50(56:62), turn.
Work on this set of sts only for Right Front.
Cont without shaping until work measures
34(37:40)cm/13½(14½:15¾)in from beg, end-
ing with a right side row.

### *Shape Neck*
**Next row** Patt to last 20(20:22) sts and slip
these 20(20:22) sts onto a safety pin, turn.
Cont without shaping on rem 30(36:40) sts until
work measures 38(41:44)cm/15(16:17¼)in from
beg, ending with a wrong side row. Leave these
sts on a spare needle.
With right side facing, slip next 12 sts onto a

holder, rejoin yarn to rem sts and patt 95(107: 119) sts, turn.

Work on this set of sts only for Back. Cont without shaping until work measures same as Right Front, ending with a wrong side row. Leave these sts on a spare needle.

With right side facing, slip next 12 sts onto a holder, rejoin yarn to rem 50 (56:62) sts for Left Front, patt to end.

Complete to match Right Front, reversing neck shaping.

### Join Shoulders

With right sides of Back and Fronts together, cast off together 30(36:40) shoulder sts (see diagram page 39), leaving centre 35(35:39) back neck sts on a holder.

### SLEEVES

With set of four 2¼mm (No 13/US 4) needles, M and right side facing, slip first 6 sts from holder at one armhole edge onto a safety pin,

rejoin yarn to next st, K6, pick up and K96(99:108) sts evenly around armhole edge, K across sts on a safety pin. 108(111:120) sts. Mark end of last round to denote end of rounds. K 2 rounds. Work in rounds of st st (every round K) and patt from chart as follows:

**1st and 3rd sizes only**
**1st round** Rep 12 sts of 2nd(24th) row of chart 9(10) times.
**2nd round:** Rep 12 sts of 1st(23rd) row of chart 9(10) times.

**2nd size only**
**1st round** Work 1st edge st of 14th row of chart, then rep 12 sts 9 times, work last 2 edge sts.
**2nd round** Work 1st edge st of 13th row of chart, then rep 12 sts 9 times, work last 2 edge sts.

**All sizes**
These 2 rows set position of patt. Cont in patt as set, working rows from chart in reverse

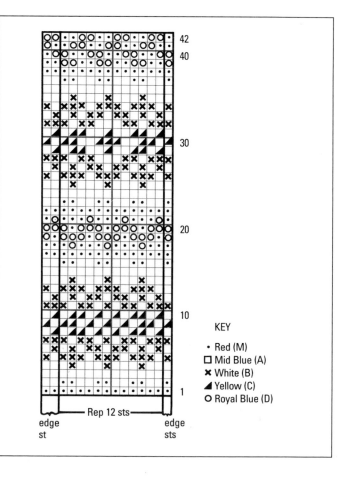

KEY

• Red (M)
☐ Mid Blue (A)
✖ White (B)
◢ Yellow (C)
○ Royal Blue (D)

— Rep 12 sts —

edge st        edge sts

order, **at the same time**, dec one st at each end of 18th(8th:10th) round and every foll 3rd(4th:4th) round until 62(65:70) sts rem. With M, K 1 round.

**Next round** With M, K2(5:4), [K2 tog, K8(10:9) sts] to end. 56(60:64) sts.
Change to set of four 2mm (No 14/US 2) needles.

**1st to 6th rounds** [K2C, M yarn forward, P2M, M yarn back] to end.

**7th to 12th rounds** Work 1st to 6th rounds, but using B instead of C.

**13th to 18th rounds** Work 1st to 6th rounds. With M, work 1 round in rib. Cast off in rib.

## NECKBAND

With 2mm (No 14/US 2) needles, M and right side facing, [K4(4:5), K2 tog, K4] twice across sts on a safety pin at Right Front neck, pick up and K 13 sts up right front neck, K back neck sts dec 3 sts evenly, pick up and K 13 sts down left front neck, then [K4, K2 tog, K4(4:5)] twice across sts on a safety pin. 94(94:102) sts. Work as follows:

**1st row (wrong side)** K2, [P2, K2] to end.
**2nd row** P2M, M yarn back, [K2C, M yarn forward, P2M, M yarn back] to end.
**3rd row** K2M, M yarn forward, [P2C, M yarn back, K2M, M yarn forward] to end.
**4th and 5th rows** As 2nd and 3rd rows.
**6th to 8th rows** Work 2nd and 3rd rows, then work 2nd row again, but using B instead of C.
**9th row** As 3rd row.
**10th row** As 2nd row.
**11th row** With M, as 1st row.
Cast off in rib.

## BUTTONHOLE BAND

With 2mm (No 14/US 2) needles, M and right side facing, pick up and K87(93:99) sts evenly along front edge of Right Front to top of neckband. Work in patt as follows:

**1st row** K1, [P1, K1] to end.
This row forms patt. Patt 4 rows more.
**1st buttonhole row** Patt 4, [cast off 2, patt 10(11:12) sts more] 6 times, cast off 2, patt to end.
**2nd buttonhole row** Patt to end, casting on 2 sts over those cast off in previous row.
Patt 4 more rows. P 1 row. Cast off knitwise.

## BUTTON BAND

Work to match Buttonhole Band omitting buttonholes.

## TO COMPLETE

Hand wash in lukewarm water. Pat dry in towel. Stretch out to size and shape and dry flat away from heat or sunlight. Sew on buttons when dry.

## BERET

With set of four 2mm (No 14/US 2) needles and M, cast on 134 sts. Mark end of cast on row to denote ends of rounds. Taking care not to twist the work, cont in rounds of K1, P1 rib for 15 rounds.
**Next round** K4, [K twice in next st, K12] to end. 144 sts.
Change to set of four 2¼mm (No 13/US 4) needles. K 2 rounds.

Work in rounds of st st (every round K) and patt from chart as follows:

**1st round** Rep 12 sts of 1st row of chart 12 times.

**2nd to 16th rounds** Rep 1st round fifteen times more, but working 2nd to 16th row of chart.

**17th round** With M, [K twice in next st, K11] to end. 156 sts.

**18th to 37th rounds** Rep 12 sts 13 times across each round, work 18th to 37th row of chart. With M, K 1 round.

**Next round** With M, [K2 tog, K11] to end. 144 sts.

With M, K 1 round.

### *Shape Crown*

**1st round** [1D, 5M] to end.

**2nd round** [2D, 3M, 1D] to end.

**3rd round** [1M, 2D, 3M, 1D, 3M, 2D] to end.

**4th round** [2M, 2D, 5M, 2D, 1M] to end.

**5th round** [1A, 2M, 2A, 3M, 2A, 2M] to end.

**6th round** [2A, 2M, 2A, 1M, 2A, 2M, 1A] to end.

**7th round** [1M, 2A, 2M, 3A, 2M, 1A, with A, sl 1, K2 tog, psso, 1A, 2M, 3A, 2M, 2A] to end.

**8th round** [2M, 2A, 2M, 1A, 2M, 2A, 1M, 2A, 2M, 1A, 2M, 2A, 1M] to end.

**9th round** [1A, 2M, 2A, 3M, 2A, with M, sl 1, K2 tog, psso, 2A, 3M, 2A, 2M] to end.

**10th round** [2C, 2M, 2C, 1M, 2C, 1M, 1C, 1M, 2C, 1M, 2C, 2M, 1C] to end.

**11th round** [1M, 2C, 2M, 3C, 1M, with M, sl 1, K2 tog, psso, 1M, 3C, 2M, 2C] to end.

**12th round** [2M, 2C, 2M, 1C, 2M, 1C, 2M, 1C, 2M, 2C, 1M] to end.

**13th round** [1C, 2M, 2C, 3M, with M, sl 1, K2 tog, psso, 3M, 2C, 2M] to end.

**14th round** [2C, 2M, 2C, 2M, 1C, 2M, 2C, 2M, 1C] to end.

**15th round** [1M, 2B, 2M, 2B, with M, sl 1, K2 tog, psso, 2B, 2M, 2B] to end.

**16th round** [2M, 2B, 2M, 3B, 2M, 2B, 1M] to end.

**17th round** [1B, 2M, 2B, 1M, with M, sl 1, K2 tog, psso, 1M, 2B, 2M] to end.

**18th round** [2B, 2M, 2B, 1M, 2B, 2M, 1B] to end.

**19th round** [1M, 2B, 2M, with B, sl 1, K2 tog, psso, 2M, 2B] to end.

**20th round** [2M, 2B, 3M, 2B, 1M] to end.

**21st round** [1B, 2M, 1B, with B, sl 1, K 2 tog, psso, 1B, 2M] to end.

**22nd round** [2B, 2M, 1B, 2M, 1B] to end.

**23rd round** [1M, 2B, with M, sl 1, K2 tog, psso, 2B] to end.

**24th round** [2M, with B, sl 1, K2 tog, psso, 1M] to end.

**25th round** With M, [K1, sl 1, K2 tog, psso] to end.

**26th round** With M, [K2 tog] to end.

Break off yarn, thread end through rem sts, pull up and secure.

Run a gathering thread around cast on edge. Hand wash in lukewarm water. Pat dry in towel. Place beret over large plate and pull thread around cast on edge. Leave it to dry away from heat or sunlight. Remove from plate when dry, discard thread.

# MAN'S FAIR ISLE WAISTCOAT

---◆---

## MATERIALS

2(2:2:3) 2oz hanks of Jamieson and
Smith Shetland 2 ply Jumper Weight in
Light Grey (203) M.
2×1oz hanks of same in each of White
(1) and Light Blue (33).
1×1oz hank of same in each of Dark
Blue (135), Royal Blue (FC48), Mauve
(FC37), Dark Grey (54), Mid Blue
(FC47) and Navy (36).
One 2¾mm (No 12/US 2) circular
needle, 50cm long.
One 3¼mm (No 10/US 4) circular
needle, 100cm long.
7 buttons.

## MEASUREMENTS

To fit chest 97(102:107:112)cm
38(40:42:44)in
All round at chest 104(109:114:119)cm
41(43:45:47)in
Length to shoulder 65(66:67:68)cm
25½(26:26½:26¾)in

## TENSION

29 sts and 29 rows to 10cm/4in square
measured over patt on 3¼mm (No 10/
US 4) needles.

## ABBREVIATIONS

See page 8.

## NOTE

When working in patt from chart, read
K rows from right to left and P rows
from left to right.
Strand yarn not in use loosely across
wrong side to keep fabric elastic.

## MAIN PART

WORKED IN ONE PIECE TO ARMHOLES

With 2¾mm (No 12/US 2) circular needle and
M, cast on 223(233:243:253) sts.
Work backwards and forwards as follows:
**1st row (right side)** K1, [P1, K1] to end.
**2nd row** P1, [K1, P1] to end.
Rep these 2 rows until work measures 8cm/3in
from beg, ending with a right side row.
**Next row** Inc in first st, rib 3(5:7:9), [inc in
next st, rib 2] to last 3(5:7:9) sts, rib to last st,
inc in last st. 297(309:321:333) sts.
Change to 3¼mm (No 10/US 4) circular
needle.
Beg with a K row and working in st st throughout, work patt from chart until work measures
40(40:41:41)cm/15¾(15¾:16:16)in from beg,
ending with a wrong side row.

### Divide work as follows

**Next row** Patt 2, K2 tog tbl, patt 57(59:61:63),
turn.
Work on this set of sts only for Right Front.
**Next row** Patt to end.
**Next row** Patt to last 3 sts, K2 tog, patt 1.
**Next row** Patt to end.
**Next row** Patt 2, K2 tog tbl, patt to last 3 sts,
K2 tog, patt 1.
Rep last 4 rows 3 times more. 48(50:52:54) sts.
**Next 3 rows** Patt to end.
**Next row** Patt 2, K2 tog tbl, patt to end.
Rep last 4 rows until 36(38:39:41) sts rem.
Cont without shaping until work measures
65(66:67:68)cm/25½(26:26½:26¾)in from beg,
ending with a wrong side row and dec one st
at end of last row. 35(37:38:40) sts. Leave these
sts on a spare needle.
With right side facing, slip next 20(22:24:26) sts
onto a holder, rejoin yarn to rem sts and patt
135(139:143:147) sts, turn.
Work on this set of sts only for Back.
**Next row** Patt to end.
**Next row** Patt 1, K2 tog tbl, patt to last 3 sts,
K2 tog, patt 1.
Rep last 2 rows 7 times more. 119(123:127:131)
sts.

Cont without shaping until work measures 2 rows less than Right Front, ending with a wrong side row.

### Shape Neck
**Next row** Patt 35(37:38:40), K2 tog, turn.
**Next row** P2 tog, patt to end. 35(37:38:40) sts.
Leave these sts on a spare needle.
With right side facing, slip centre 45(45:47:47) Back neck sts onto a holder, rejoin yarn to rem sts, K2 tog, patt to end.
**Next row** Patt to last 2 sts, P2 tog. 35(37:38:40) sts.
Leave these sts on a spare needle.
With right side facing, slip next 20(22:24:26) sts onto a holder, rejoin yarn to rem sts for Left Front and patt to last 4 sts, K2 tog, patt 2.
**Next row** Patt to end.
**Next row** Patt 1, K2 tog tbl, patt to end.
**Next row** Patt to end.
**Next row** Patt 1, K2 tog tbl, patt to last 4 sts, K2 tog, patt 2.
Rep last 4 rows 3 times more. 48(50:52:54) sts.
**Next 3 rows** Patt to end.

**Next row** Patt to last 4 sts, K2 tog, patt 2.
Rep last 4 rows until 36(38:39:41) sts rem.
Cont without shaping until work measures same as Right Front, ending with a wrong side row and dec one st at beg of last row. 35(37:38:40) sts.

### Join Shoulders
With right sides of Back and Fronts together, cast off together 35(37:38:40) shoulder sts (see diagram page 39).

## ARMBANDS
With 2¾mm (No 12/US 2) circular needle, M and right side facing, slip first 10(11:12:13) sts from holder at one armhole edge onto a safety pin, rejoin yarn to rem sts, K1(2:0:1), [K2 tog, K1] 3(3:4:4) times across rem sts, pick up and K108(114:114:120) sts evenly around armhole edge, K1(2:0:1), [K2 tog, K1] 3(3:4:4) times across sts on a safety pin. 122(130:130:138) sts. Work 11 rounds in K1, P1 rib. Cast off in rib.

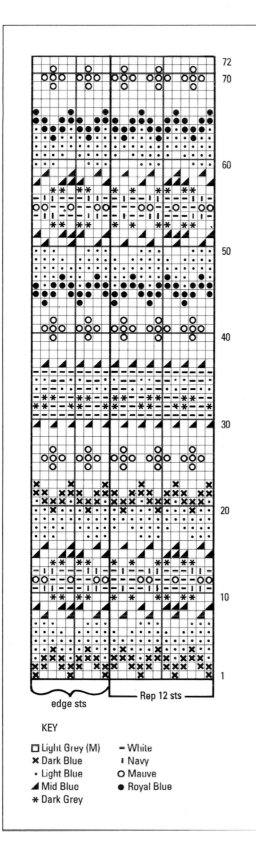

Rep 12 sts

edge sts

KEY

□ Light Grey (M)  − White
✗ Dark Blue  ı Navy
• Light Blue  ○ Mauve
◣ Mid Blue  ● Royal Blue
✶ Dark Grey

## FRONT BAND

With 2¾mm (No 12/US 2) circular needle, M and right side facing, pick up and K20 sts up Right Front welt, working between 2nd and 3rd st pick up and K64(64:68:68) sts along straight edge to beg of front shaping, 50(53:53:56) sts along shaped edge to shoulder, 2 sts down right back neck, K across 45(45:47:47) sts on back neck dec 8 sts evenly, pick up and K2 sts up left back neck, working between 2nd and 3rd st pick up and K50(53:53:56) sts along shaped edge of Left Front, 64(64:68:68) sts along straight edge to welt, pick up and K 20 sts along welt. 309(315:325:331) sts. Work backwards and forwards as follows:

**Next row** K1, [P1, K1] to end.

This row forms patt. Patt 3 more rows.

**Buttonhole row** Patt 3, [P2 tog, yrn, patt 11, K2 tog, yf, patt 11] 3 times, P2 tog, yrn, patt to end.

Patt 6 more rows. Cast off loosely in patt.

## TO COMPLETE

Fold back the 2 stitch edge on wrong side of fronts and neatly buttonhole stitch in place. Hand wash in lukewarm water. Pat dry in towel. Stretch out to size and shape and dry flat away from heat or sunlight. Sew on buttons when dry.

## MATERIALS

*Cardigan* 2(3:3) 2oz hanks of Jamieson and Smith Shetland 2 ply Jumper Weight in Cream (1a) M.
1(1:2) 2oz hanks of same in each of Dark Fawn (78) A and Light Brown (4) B.
1×2oz hanks of same in each of Light Fawn (202) C, Light Grey (203) D and Shetland Black (5) E.
1(1:2) 1oz hanks of same in Dark Grey (54) F.
1×1oz hank of same in Mid Grey (27) G.
*Beret* Small amounts of Jamieson and Smith Shetland 2 ply Jumper Weight in each of 8 colours (M, A, B, C, D, E, F and G).
One in each of 2mm (No 14/US 1) and 2¾mm (No 12/US 3) circular needles.
Set of four in each of 2mm (No 14/US 1) and 2¾mm (No 12/US 3) double pointed knitting needles.
1 pair in each of 2mm (No 14/US 1) and 2¾mm (No 12/US 3) knitting needles.
7 buttons.

## MEASUREMENTS

To fit bust 81–87(91–97:102–107)cm
32–34(36–38:40–42)in
All round at bust 98(109:121)cm
38½(43:47½)in
Length to shoulder 62(63:64)cm
24½(24¾:25¼)in
Sleeve length 53cm/21in

## TENSION

31 sts and 31 rows to 10cm/4in square measured over patt on 2¾mm (No 12/US 3) needles.

## ABBREVIATIONS

See page 8.

## NOTE

The stitches shown on charts do not include stitches decreased when shaping armholes or sleeves.
When working in patt from chart, read K rounds or rows from right to left and P rows from left to right.
Strand yarn not in use loosely across wrong side to keep fabric elastic.

# FAIR ISLE V-NECK CARDIGAN AND BERET

## *CARDIGAN*

### POCKET LININGS

MAKE 2

With 2¾mm (No 12/US 3) needles and M, cast on 29 sts. Beg with a K row and working in st st throughout, work patt from chart 1, then chart 2 as indicated for pocket lining and chart 1 again. Leave these sts on a holder.

### MAIN PART

WORKED IN ONE PIECE TO ARMHOLES

With 2mm (No 14/US 1) circular needle and M, cast on 226(258:290) sts. Work backwards and forwards as follows:
**1st row** K2, [P2, K2] to end.
**2nd row (right side)** P2M, M yarn back, [K2A, M yarn forward, P2M, M yarn back] to end.
**3rd row** K2M, M yarn forward, [P2A, M yarn back, K2M, M yarn forward] to end.
**4th row** As 2nd row.
**5th to 7th rows** Using G instead of A, work 3rd row, then 2nd and 3rd rows.
**8th and 9th rows** Using B instead of A, work 2nd and 3rd rows.
**10th row** Using E instead of A, work 2nd row.
**11th and 12th rows** Using B instead of A, work 3rd row, then 2nd row.
**13th to 15th rows** As 5th to 7th rows.
**16th to 18th rows** As 2nd to 4th rows.
**Next row** With M, P8(8:12), ★[inc in next st, P3] 3(3:5) times, inc in each of next 2 sts, P2, [inc in next st, P3] 0(2:2) times; rep from ★ to last 10(10:22) sts, [inc in next st, P3] 2(1:3) times, P2(6:10). 293(329:365) sts.
Change to 2¾mm (No 12/US 3) circular needle.
Beg with a K row and working in st st throughout, work patt from charts as follows:
**1st to 5th rows** Work 1st to 5th rows of chart 1.
**6th to 26th rows** Work 1st to 21st rows of chart 2.

**27th to 31st rows** Work 1st to 5th rows of chart 1.

**32nd row** Work 1st row of 1st repeat of chart 3 placing pockets as follows: patt 24, sl next 29 sts onto a holder, patt across sts of first pocket lining, patt to last 53 sts, sl next 29 sts onto a holder, patt across sts of second pocket lining, patt to end.

**33rd to 41st rows** Work 2nd to 10th rows of 1st repeat of chart 3.

**42nd to 46th rows** Using B instead of F, work 1st to 5th rows of chart 1.

**47th to 67th rows** Work 1st to 21st rows of chart 4.

**68th to 72nd rows** As 42nd to 46th rows.

**73rd to 82nd rows** Work 1st to 10th rows of 2nd rep of chart 3.

These 82 rows form patt. Cont in patt, omitting pocket placing and working appropriate repeats of chart 2, chart 3 and chart 4 until work measures 35cm/13¾in from beg, ending with a wrong side row.

### Shape Fronts

**Next row** Patt 2, K2 tog tbl, patt to last 4 sts, K2 tog, patt 2.

**Next 2 rows** Patt to end.

**Next row** Patt 2, P2 tog, patt to last 4 sts, P2 tog tbl, patt 2.

**Next 2 rows** Patt to end.

Rep last 6 rows twice more. 281(317:353) sts.

### Divide work as follows

**Next row** Patt 2, K2 tog tbl, patt 54(62:70), turn.

Work on this set of sts only for Right Front.

**1st row** Patt to end.

**2nd row** Patt to last 3 sts, K2 tog, patt 1.

**3rd row** Patt to last 4 sts, P2 tog tbl, patt 2.

**4th row** Patt to last 3 sts, K2 tog, patt 1.

**5th row** Patt to end.

**6th row** Patt 2, K2 tog tbl, patt to last 3 sts, K2 tog, patt 1.

Rep these 6 rows once more, then work 1st to 4th rows again. 44(52:60) sts. Keeping armhole edge straight, cont dec at front edge one st inside the border of 2 sts as before on every 3rd row until 31(38:45) sts rem.

Cont without shaping until work measures 62(63:64)cm/24½(24¾:25¼)in from beg, ending with a wrong side row. Leave these sts on a spare needle.

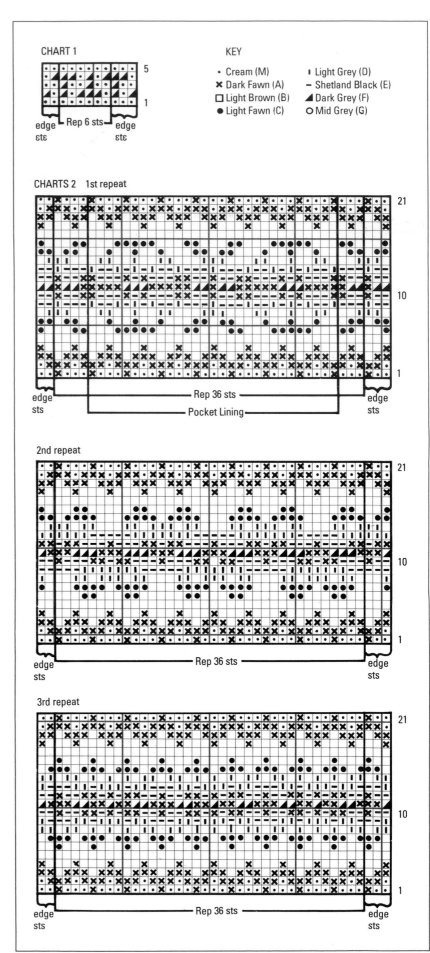

CHART 1

KEY
- • Cream (M)
- ✖ Dark Fawn (A)
- ☐ Light Brown (B)
- ● Light Fawn (C)
- ┃ Light Grey (D)
- – Shetland Black (E)
- ◣ Dark Grey (F)
- ○ Mid Grey (G)

└ Rep 6 sts ┘

edge sts    edge sts

CHARTS 2   1st repeat

Rep 36 sts

Pocket Lining

edge sts    edge sts

2nd repeat

Rep 36 sts

edge sts    edge sts

3rd repeat

Rep 36 sts

edge sts    edge sts

CHARTS 3  1st repeat

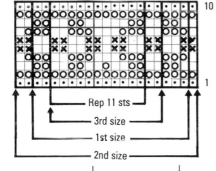

10

1

Rep 11 sts
3rd size
1st size
2nd size

2nd repeat

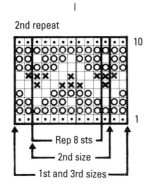

10

1

Rep 8 sts
2nd size
1st and 3rd sizes

3rd repeat

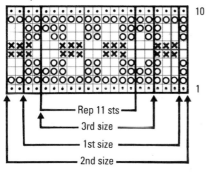

10

1

Rep 11 sts
3rd size
1st size
2nd size

4th repeat

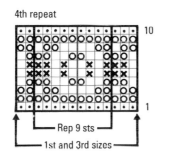

10

1

Rep 9 sts
1st and 3rd sizes

CHARTS 4  1st repeat

21

10

1

edge
sts

Rep 36 sts

edge
sts

2nd repeat

21

10

1

edge
sts

Rep 36 sts

edge
sts

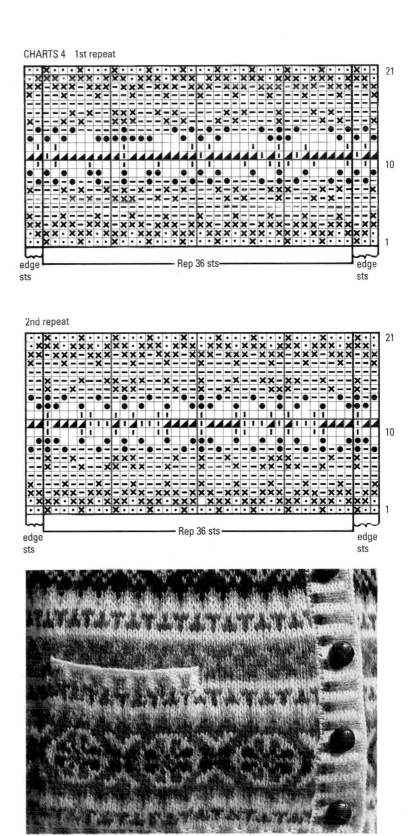

With right side facing, slip first 20(22:24) sts onto a holder, rejoin yarn to rem sts and patt 125(141:157) sts, turn. Work on this set of sts only for Back.

**1st row** Patt to end.

**2nd row** Patt 1, K2 tog tbl, patt to last 3 sts, K2 tog, patt 1.

Rep last 2 rows 7 times more. 109(125:141) sts. Cont without shaping until work measures same as Right Front, ending with a wrong side row. Leave these sts on a spare needle.

With right side facing, slip first 20(22:24) sts onto a holder, rejoin yarn to rem sts for Left Front, patt to last 4 sts, K2 tog, patt 2.

**1st row** Patt to end.

**2nd row** Patt 1, K2 tog tbl, patt to end.

**3rd row** Patt 2, P2 tog, patt to end.

**4th row** Patt 1, K2 tog tbl, patt to end.

**5th row** Patt to end.

**6th row** Patt 1, K2 tog tbl, patt to last 4 sts, K2 tog, patt 2.

Complete to match Right Front.

### *Join Shoulders*

With right sides of Back and Fronts together, cast off together 31(38:45) shoulder sts (see diagram page 39), leaving centre 47(49:51) back neck sts on a holder.

### SLEEVES

With set of 2¾mm (No 12/US 3) needles, M and right side facing, slip first 10(11:12) sts on holder at armhole onto safety pin, rejoin yarn and K rem 10(11:12) sts, pick up and K124(127:125) sts evenly around armhole edge, K10(11:12) sts from safety pin. 144(149:149) sts. Mark end of last round to denote end of rounds. Work in rounds of st st (every round K) and patt from chart as follows:

**1st round** Work 0(3:3) edge sts of 21st row of chart 4 (2nd repeat), rep 36 sts to last 0(2:2) sts, work 0(2:2) edge sts.

**2nd to 21st round** Rep last round 20 times, but working chart 4 in reverse order from 20th to 1st row.

These 21 rounds set patt. Cont in patt as set, matching Main Part and working charts in reverse order, **at the same time**, dec one st at each end of next round and every foll 5th round until 112(117:117) sts rem, then on every foll 4th round until 86(91:91) sts rem.

**Next round** With M, K5(6:6), [K2 tog, K1] to last 3(4:4) sts, K3(4:4). 60(64:64) sts.

Change to set of four 2mm (No 14/US 1) needles.

**1st to 3rd rounds** [P2M, M yarn back, K2A, M yarn forward] to end.

**4th to 6th rounds** Using G instead of A, work 1st to 3rd rounds.

**7th and 8th rounds** Using B instead of A, work 1st and 2nd rounds.

**9th round** Using E instead of A, work 1st round.

**10th and 11th rounds** Work 7th and 8th rounds.

**12th to 14th rounds** Work 4th to 6th rounds.

**15th to 17th rounds** Work 1st to 3rd rounds.

With M, rib 1 round. Cast off in rib.

### FRONT BAND

With 2mm (No 14/US 1) circular needle, M and right side facing, pick up and K 112 sts evenly along straight edge of Right Front picking up sts between 2nd and 3rd st, 80(82:84) sts along shaped edge to shoulder, K across 47(49:51) sts on back neck dec 5(3:5) sts evenly, pick up and K 80(82:84) sts down shaped edge of Left Front to beg of front shaping and 112 sts down straight edge. 426(434:438) sts. Work 9th to 18th rows of rib as given for Main Part, working buttonholes on 4th and 5th of these 10 rows as follows:

**1st buttonhole row** Rib 8, [cast off 1, rib 16 including st used in casting off] 7 times, rib to end.

**2nd buttonhole row** Rib to end, casting on 1 st over the one cast off in previous row.

With M, rib 1 row. Cast off in rib.

### POCKET TOPS

With 2mm (No 14/US 1) needles, M and right side facing, work across sts of one pocket top as follows:

**1st row** [P2M, M yarn back, K2A, M yarn forward] 7 times, with M, P twice in next st. Work a further 3 rows in rib as set. With M, rib 1 row. Cast off in rib.

### TO COMPLETE

Catch down pocket linings and sides of pocket tops. Fold back the 2 stitch edge on wrong side of fronts and neatly stitch in place. Hand wash in lukewarm water. Pat dry in towel. Stretch out to size and shape and dry flat away from heat or sunlight. Sew on buttons when dry.

## BERET

With set of four 2¾mm (No 12/US 3) needles and M, cast on 120 sts. Mark end of cast on row to denote end of rounds. Taking care not to twist the work, cont in rounds as follows:

**1st round** [P2, K2] to end.

**2nd to 4th rounds** [P2M, M yarn back, K2A, M yarn forward] to end.

**5th to 7th rounds** [P2M, M yarn back, K2G, M yarn foward] to end.

**8th and 9th rounds** [P2M, M yarn back, K2B, M yarn foward] to end.

**10th round** [P2M, M yarn back, K2E, M yarn forward] to end.

**11th round** As 8th round.

**Next round** With M, *[inc in next st, K3] 3 times, inc in next st, K7; rep from * to end. 144 sts. K 1 round in M.

**1st round** Rep 36 sts 4 times of 1st row of chart 2 (1st repeat).

**2nd to 21st rounds** Rep 1st round 20 times, but working 2nd to 21st rows of chart 2.

**22nd round** With M, K4, *inc in next st, K3, [inc in next st, K2] twice; rep from * to end. 186 sts.

**23rd round** Rep 6 sts of 2nd row of chart 1 to end.

**24th to 26th rounds** Rep 23rd round 3 times, but working 3rd to 5th rows of chart 1 and dec 10 sts evenly across last round. 176 sts.

**27th round** Rep 11 sts of 1st row of chart 3 (1st repeat) to end.

**28th to 36th rounds** Rep 27th round 9 times, but working 2nd to 10th rows of chart 3 and dec 8 sts evenly across last round. 168 sts.

**37th round** Rep 6 sts of 1st row of chart 1 to end.

**38th to 41st rounds** Using B instead of F, rep 37th round 4 times, but working 2nd to 5th rows of chart 1 and dec 8 sts evenly across last round. 160 sts.

**Next round** [K1G, 4M] to end.

**Next round** [K 1M, 1G, 7M, 1G] to end.

**Next round** K [1G, 1M, 1G, 5M, 1G, with M, sl 1, K2 tog, psso, 1G, 5M, 1G, 1M] to end.

**Next round** * [K 1M, 1G] twice, 3M, [1G, 1M] 3 times, 2M, 1G, 1M, 1G; rep from * to end.

**Next round** [K 1F, 1C, 1F, 3C, 1F, 1C, with C, sl 1, K2 tog, psso, 1C, 1F, 3C, 1F, 1C] to end.

**Next round** [K 1C, 1F, 3C, 1F, 2C, 1F, 2C, 1F, 3C, 1F] to end.

**Next round** [K 1F, 3C, 1F, 2C, with C, sl 1, K2 tog, psso, 2C, 1F, 3C] to end.

**Next round** [K 3C, 1F, 3C, 1F, 3C, 1F, 2C] to end.

**Next round** [K 2D, 1B, 3D, with D, sl 1, K2 tog, psso, 3D, 1B, 1D] to end.

**Next round** [K 1D, 1B, 4D, 1B, 4D, 1B] to end.

**Next round** [K 1D, 1B, 3D, with D, sl 1, K2 tog, psso, 3D, 1B] to end.

**Next round** [K 1D, 1B, 3D, 1B, 3D, 1B] to end.

**Next round** [K 1A, 1E, 2A, with A, sl 1, K2 tog, psso, 2A, 1E] to end.

**Next round** [K 1A, 1E, 2A, 1E, 2A, 1E] to end.

**Next round** [K 1A, 1E, 1A, with A, sl 1, K 2 tog, psso, 1A, 1E] to end.

**Next round** [K 1A, 1E] to end.

**Next round** [K 1G, 1B, with G, sl 1, K2 tog, psso, 1B] to end.

**Next round** [K 1G, 1B] to end.

**Next round** [K 1G, with B, sl 1, K2 tog, psso] to end.

**Next round** [K 1G, 1B] to end.

Break off yarn, thread end through rem sts, pull up and secure.

Run a gathering thread around cast on edge. Hand wash in lukewarm water. Pat dry in towel. Place beret over large plate and pull thread around cast on edge. Leave it to dry away from heat or sunlight. Remove from plate when dry, discard thread.

## MATERIALS

8(8:9) 1oz hanks of Jamieson and Smith
Shetland 2 ply Jumper Weight in Grey
(27) M.
1×1oz hank of same in each of Blue
(16), Rust (125), White (1) and Yellow
(23).
One in each of 3mm (No 11/US 3) and
3¾mm (No 9/US 5) circular needles,
80cm long.
One set of four in each of 3mm (No 11/
US 3) and 3¾mm (No 9/US 5) double
pointed knitting needles.

## MEASUREMENTS

To fit chest 91(97-102:107-112)cm
36(38-40:42-44)in
All round at chest 102(111:120)cm
40(43¾:47¼)in
Length to shoulder 68(69:70)cm
26¾(27:27½)in

## TENSION

26 sts and 34 rows to 10cm/4in square
measured over st st on 3¾mm (No 9/
US 5) needles.

## ABBREVIATIONS

See page 8.

## NOTE

When working in patt, read every row
of chart from right to left. Strand yarn
not in use loosely across wrong side to
keep fabric elastic.

# MAN'S SLIPOVER WITH FAIR ISLE BORDER

## MAIN PART

WORKED IN ONE PIECE TO ARMHOLES

With 3mm (No 11/US 3) circular needle and
M, cast on 264(288:312) sts. Mark end of cast
on row to denote end of rounds. Taking care
not to twist the work, cont in rounds of K1, P1
rib for 3 cm/1¼in.
Change to 3¾mm (No 9/US 5) circular needle.
Work in st st (every round K) for 12 rounds.
Now work border patt from chart until 29
rounds of patt have been worked.
Cont in M and st st only until work measures
44cm/17¼in from beg.

### Shape Armholes

**Next row** K10(12:14) and sl these sts onto a
safety pin, K112(120:128) sts, sl next 10(12:14)
sts onto a safety pin, turn. Work backwards
and forwards on this set of sts only for Back.
**Next row** P.
**Next row** K1, K2 tog, K to last 3 sts, sl 1, K1,
psso, K1.
Rep last 2 rows 9 times more. 92(100:108) sts.
Cont in st st without shaping until work
measures 67(68:69)cm/26½(26¾:27¼)in from
beg, ending with a P row.

### Shape Neck

**Next row** K28(30:32), turn. Work on this set
of sts only.
Dec one st at neck edge on next 3 rows. Leave
rem 25(27:29) sts on a spare needle.
With right side facing, slip centre 36(40:44)
Back sts onto a holder, rejoin yarn to rem sts
and K to end. Complete to match first side.

### Shape Armhole and Neck

With right side facing, rejoin yarn to rem sts,
K10(12:14) and sl these sts onto a safety pin,
K53(57:61), sl 1, K1, psso, K1, turn.
★★ Work backwards and forwards on this set
of sts only for first side of front neck.
**Next row** P.

**Next row** K1, K2 tog, K to last 3 sts, sl 1, K1, psso, K1.

Rep last 2 rows 3(5:7) times more. ★★

**Next row** P.

**Next row** K1, K2 tog, K to end.

**Next row** P.

**Next row** K1, K2 tog, K to last 3 sts, sl 1, K1, psso, K1.

Rep last 4 rows 2(1:0) times more.

**Next row** P.

**Next row** K.

**Next row** P.

**Next row** K to last 3 sts, sl 1, K1, psso, K1.

Rep last 4 rows until 25(27:29) sts rem.

Cont in st st without shaping until work measures same as Back, ending with a P row. Leave these sts on a spare needle.

### Shape Armhole and Neck

With right side facing, rejoin yarn to rem sts for other side of front neck, K to last 10(12:14) sts and sl these onto a safety pin, turn.

Work as given from ★★ to ★★.

**Next row** P.

**Next row** K to last 3 sts, sl 1, K1, psso, K1.

**Next row** P.

**Next row** K1, K2 tog, K to last 3 sts, sl 1, K1, psso, K1.

Rep last 4 rows 2(1:0) times more.

**Next row** P.

**Next row** K.

**Next row** P.

**Next row** K1, K2 tog, K to end.

Complete to match first side.

### Join Shoulders

With right side facing, graft each shoulder sts together (see diagram on page 39).

### NECKBAND

With set of four 3¾mm (No 9/US 5) needles and M, pick up and K66(69:72) sts up right front neck, 3 sts down right back neck, K across centre 36(40:44) back neck sts dec 3 sts evenly, pick up and K3 sts up left back neck and 66(69:72) sts down left front neck. 171(181:191) sts. Mark end of last round. Work in rounds of st st and patt from chart as follows:

**1st round** Work last 7(0:5) sts of 11th row of chart, rep 12 sts 13(15:15) times, then work first 8(1:6) sts.

This round sets patt.

**Next round** K2 tog, patt to last 2 sts, K2 tog tbl.

Rep last round 7 times.

Change to set of four 3mm (No 11/US 3) needles. Cont in M, K 1 round dec as before.

**Next round** K2 tog, [P1, K1] to last 3 sts, P1, K2 tog tbl.

**Next round** P2 tog, [K1, P1] to last 3 sts, K1, P2 tog tbl.

Cast off in rib dec as before.

### ARMBANDS

With set of four 3mm (No 11/US 3) needles and right side facing, rejoin M yarn to sts on 2nd safety pin at one armhole edge, work across these sts as follows: K2(3:4), K2 tog, K2, K2

tog, K2(3:4), pick up and K90(96:102) sts evenly around armhole edge, K2(3:4), K2 tog, K2, K2 tog, K2(3:4) across sts on first safety pin. 106(116:126) sts. Work 8 rounds in K1, P1 rib. Cast off loosely in rib.

### TO COMPLETE

Hand wash in lukewarm water. Pat dry in towel. Stretch out to size and shape and dry flat away from heat or sunlight.

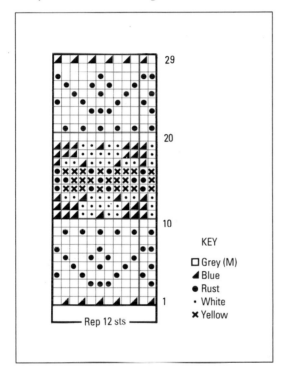

29

20

10

1

KEY

□ Grey (M)
◢ Blue
● Rust
· White
✕ Yellow

— Rep 12 sts —

### GRAFTING

Place pieces to be grafted as shown on diagram. Insert needle purlwise in end st of bottom piece, then in end st of top piece. ★ Reinsert needle knitwise in bottom st, then insert purlwise in next st (A), reinsert needle knitwise in top st, insert purlwise in next st (B); rep from ★ until all sts are worked off, keeping grafted sts at same tension as the knitting.

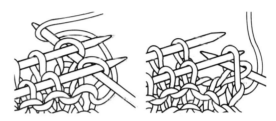

### CASTING OFF SHOULDERS TOGETHER

K into first st of both needles together (A), ★ K into next st on both needles together, then pass 2nd st on right-hand needle over 1st st (B); rep from ★ until all sts are worked off. Fasten off.

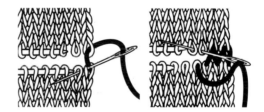

## MATERIALS

8(8:9) 1oz hanks of Jamieson and
Smith Shetland 2 ply Jumper Weight in
Navy (21) M.
3(3:4) 1oz hanks of same in Red (125) A.
3(4:4) 1oz hanks of same in Gold (28).
1(1:2) 2oz hanks of same in Cream (1a).
2(2:2) 1oz hanks of same in Blue (142).
1 pair in each of 2¾mm (No 12/US 2)
and 3¼ mm (No 10/US 4) knitting
needles.
One set of four in each of 2¾mm
(No 12/US 2) and 3¼mm (No 10/
US 4) double pointed knitting needles.

## MEASUREMENTS

To fit bust 81–86(91–97:102–107)cm
32–34(36–38:40–42)in
All round at bust 108(116:124)cm
42½(45½:48¾)in
Length to shoulder 64(68:68)cm
25¼(26¾:26¾)in
Sleeve seam 47cm/18½in

## TENSION

29 sts and 29 rows to 10cm/4in square
measured over patt on 3¼mm (No 10/
US 4) needles.

## ABBREVIATIONS

See page 8.

## NOTE

When working patt from chart, read K
rounds or rows from right to left and P
rows from left to right.
Strand yarn not in use loosely across
wrong side over no more than 6 sts at
the time to keep fabric elastic.

# TRADITIONAL FAIR ISLE SWEATER

❖

### BACK

With 2¾mm (No 12/US 2) needles and M, cast
on 131(141:151) sts. K 2 rows.
**Next row (wrong side)** P1M, [1A, 1M] to
end.
Work in rib patt as follows:
**1st row** K1M, [A yarn forward, P1A, A yarn
back, K1M] to end.
**2nd row** P1M, [A yarn back, K1A, A yarn
forward, P1M] to end.
Rep these 2 rows until work measures 8cm/3in
from beg, ending with a 1st row.
Change to 3¼mm (No 10/US 4) needles.
**Next row** With M, P3, m1, [P5, m1] to last 3
sts, P3. 157(169:181) sts.
Beg with a K row, work in st st and patt from
chart as follows:
**1st row (right side)** Work last 18(0:6) sts of
13th(1st:1st) row of chart, rep 24 sts 5(7:7)
times, then work first 19(1:7) sts.
**2nd row** Work last 19(1:7) sts of 14th(2nd:2nd)
row of chart, rep 24 sts 5(7:7) times, then work
first 18(0:6) sts.
These 2 rows set position of patt. Cont in patt
as set, working appropriate rows of chart until
160(172:172) rows in all have been worked in
patt.

### Shape Neck
**Next row** Patt 54(60:66), K2 tog, turn.
**Next row** P2 tog, patt to end.
Leave rem 54(60:66) sts on a spare needle.
With right side facing, slip centre 45 sts onto a
holder, rejoin yarn to rem sts, K2 tog, patt to
end.
**Next row** Patt to last 2 sts, P2 tog.
Leave rem 54(60:66) sts on a holder.

### FRONT
Work as given for Back until 140(152:152) rows
in all have been worked in patt.

### Shape Neck
**Next row** Patt 63(69:75), turn. Work on this
set of sts only.
Keeping patt correct, dec one st at neck edge on

next 9 rows. 54(60:66) sts. Patt 12 rows straight. Leave these sts on a spare needle.

With right side facing, slip centre 31 sts onto a holder, rejoin yarn to rem sts and patt to end. Complete to match first side.

### *Join Shoulders*

With right sides of Back and Front together, cast off together 54(60:66) shoulder sts (see diagram page 39).

### SLEEVES

With 2¾mm (No 12/US 2) needles and M, cast on 55(55:59) sts. K2 rows.

**Next row (wrong side)** P1M, [1A, 1M] to end.

Work in rib patt as given for Back for 7cm/2¾in, ending with a 1st row.

Change to 3¼mm (No 10/US 4) needles.

**Next row** With M, P 2(2:4), m1, [P3(3:2), m1] to last 2(2:5) sts, P2(2:5). 73(73:85) sts.

Beg with a K row, work in st st and patt from chart as follows:

**1st row (right side)** Work last 0(0:6) sts of 1st row of chart, rep 24 sts 3 times, then work first 1(1:7) sts.

**2nd row** Work last 1(1:7) sts of 2nd row of chart, rep 24 sts 3 times, then work first 0(0:6) sts.

These 2 rows set position of patt. Cont in patt as set, working appropriate rows of chart, **at the same time**, inc one st at each end of next and every foll alt row until there are 127(127:119) sts, then on every foll 3rd row until there are 161(161:165) sts, working inc sts into patt. Patt 14(14:16) rows straight. Cast off.

### NECKBAND

With set of four 3¼mm (No 10/US 4) needles, M and right side facing, pick up and K 21 sts down left front neck, K across 31 sts at centre front neck, pick up and K 21 sts up right front neck, 1 st down right back neck, K across 45 sts at centre back neck, pick up and K 1 st up left back neck. 120 sts. Working in rounds and st st (every round K), work 1st to 12th row of chart repeating 24 sts 5 times across each round.

Change to set of four 2¾mm (No 12/US 2) needles. Cont in M only. P 1 round, K 1 round, P 1 round. K15 rounds. Cast off loosely.

### TO MAKE UP

Pin pieces out to correct measurements and press with a warm iron over a damp cloth. Sew on sleeves, placing centre of sleeves to shoulder seams. Join side and sleeve seams. Fold neckband on second P round to wrong side and slip stitch in position. Press seams.

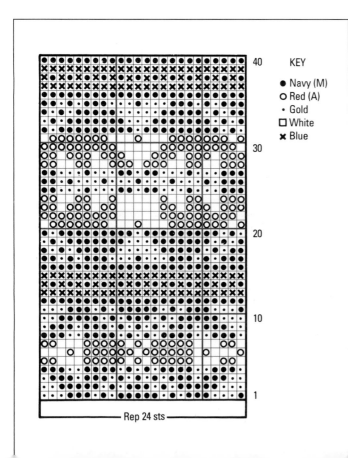

KEY

- ● Navy (M)
- ○ Red (A)
- · Gold
- □ White
- ✕ Blue

Rep 24 sts

## MATERIALS

3(4:4) 2oz hanks of Jamiesons Pure Shetland in Natural White (104) M.
2(2:3) 1oz hanks of same in Kingfisher (640).
2x1oz hanks of same in each of Gold (410), Light Red (462) and Dark Red (577).
1 pair in each of 2mm (No 14/US 1) and 2¾mm (No 12/US 3) knitting needles.
One 2mm (No 14/US 1) circular needle, 40cm long.

## MEASUREMENTS

To fit chest 97(102:107)cm/38(40:42)in
All round at chest 110(117:125)cm 43¼(46:49¼)in
Length to shoulder 69(71:73)cm 27(28:28¾)in

## TENSION

31 sts and 34 rows to 10cm/4in square measured over patt on 2¾mm (No 12/US 3) needles.

## ABBREVIATIONS

See page 8.

## NOTE

When working in patt from chart, read K rows from right to left and P rows from left to right.
Strand yarn not in use loosely across wrong side to keep fabric elastic.

# MAN'S ALL OVER FAIR ISLE SLIPOVER

---◆---

## BACK

With 2mm (No 14/US 1) needles and M, cast on 136(146:156) sts.
Work 7cm/2¾in in K1, P1 rib.
**Next row** Rib 1(2:3), [inc in next st, rib 3] to last 3(4:5) sts, inc in next st, rib to end. 170(182:194) sts.
Change to 2¾mm (No 12/US 3) needles.
Beg with a K row, work in st st and patt from chart until work measures 41(42:43)cm/16(16½:17)in from beg, ending with a wrong side row. ★★

### Shape Armholes

**Next row** Patt 9(11:13) and slip these sts onto a safety pin, patt to last 10(12:14) sts, slip last 10(12:14) sts onto a safety pin. Work on centre 151(159:167) sts only.
**Next row** Patt to end.
**Next row** K1, K2 tog, patt to last 3 sts, sl 1, K1, psso, K1.
Rep last 2 rows twice more.
**Next 3 rows** Patt to end.
**Next row** K1, K2 tog, patt to last 3 sts, sl 1, K1, psso, K1.
Rep last 4 rows 3 times more. 137(145:153) sts.
Cont without shaping until work measures 69(71:73)cm/27(28:28¾)in from beg, ending with a wrong side row. Leave these sts on a spare needle.

## FRONT

Work as given for Back to ★★.

### Shape Armhole and Neck

**Next row** Patt 9(11:13) sts and slip these sts onto a safety pin, patt 72(76:80), sl 1, K1, psso, K1, turn.
★★★Work on this set of 74(78:82) sts only.
**Next row** Patt to end.
**Next row** K1, K2 tog, patt to last 3 sts, sl 1, K1, psso, K1.
Rep last 2 rows twice more.
**Next 3 rows** Patt to end.
**Next row** K1, K2 tog, patt to last 3 sts, sl 1, K1, psso, K1.

Rep last 4 rows 3 times more. ★★★
**Next 3 rows** Patt to end.
**Next row** Patt to last 3 sts, sl 1, K1, psso, K1.
Rep last 4 rows until 44(47:50) sts rem.
Cont without shaping until work measures same as Back, ending with a wrong side row. Leave these sts on a spare needle.
With right side facing, slip centre st onto a safety pin, rejoin yarn to rem sts, K1, K2 tog, patt to last 10(12:14) sts, slip last 10(12:14) sts onto a safety pin. Work as given for first side from ★★★ to ★★★.
**Next 3 rows** Patt to end.
**Next row** K1, K2 tog, patt to end.
Complete to match first side.

### Join Shoulders
With right sides of Back and Front together, cast off together 44(47:50) shoulder sts (see diagram page 39), leaving centre 49(51:53) back neck sts on a holder.

### NECKBAND
With 2mm (No 14/US 1) circular needle, M and beg at left shoulder, pick up and K 80(84:88) sts down left front neck, K centre front st, pick up and K 80(84:88) sts up right front neck, K across 49(51:53) back neck sts dec 4 sts evenly. 206(216:226) sts. Mark end of last round to denote end of rounds.
Work in rounds as follows:
**1st round** P1, [K1, P1] to 1 st before centre front st, sl 1, K 2 tog, psso, [P1, K1] to end.
**2nd round** Rib to end.
**3rd round** Rib to 1 st before centre st, P3 tog tbl, rib to end.
**4th round** Rib to end.
Rep last 4 rounds twice more, then work 1st and 2nd rounds again. Rib 2 rounds.
**Next round** Rib to centre front st, m1, rib 1, m1, rib to end.
Rib 1 round. Rep last 2 rounds 6 times more. Cast off loosely in rib.

### ARMBANDS
With 2 mm (No 14/US 1) needles, M and right side facing, slip 9(11:13) sts from safety pin at one armhole onto needle, rejoin yarn and pick up and K 140(148:156) sts evenly around armhole edge, K10(12:14) sts from safety pin. 159(171:183) sts.
**Next row** P1, [K1, P1] to end.

**Next row** K1, [P1, K1] to end.
Rep last 2 rows 4 times more, then work the
1st of the 2 rows again. Cast off in rib.

### TO MAKE UP

Fold neckband in half to wrong side and slip
stitch in place. Join side and armband seams.
Hand wash in lukewarm water. Pat dry in
towel. Stretch out to size and shape and dry flat
away from heat and sunlight.

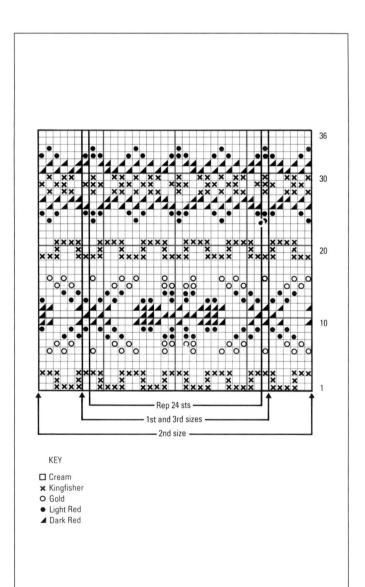

KEY

☐ Cream
✗ Kingfisher
○ Gold
● Light Red
◢ Dark Red

## MATERIALS

6(7:7) 1oz hanks of Jamiesons Pure
Shetland in Mist (180) M.
1×2oz hank of same in White (304) A.
1×1oz hank of same in each of Twilight
(175) B, Dusk (165) C, Wild Violet
(153) and Pink (550).
One in each of 3mm (No 11/US 3) and
3¾mm (No 9/US 5) circular needles,
40cm long.
Set of four in each of 3mm (No 11/
US 3) and 3¾mm (No 9/US 5) double
pointed knitting needles.

## MEASUREMENTS

To fit chest 61(66:71)cm/24(26:28)in
All round at chest 68(73:78)cm
26¾(28¾:30¾)in
Length to centre back neck 41(45:49)cm
16(17¾:19¼)in
Sleeve length (with cuff turned back)
30(33:36)cm/11¾(13:14)in

## TENSION

25 sts and 35 rows to 10cm/4in square
measured over st st on 3¾mm (No 9/
US 5) needles.

## ABBREVIATIONS

See page 8.

## NOTE

When working in patt, read every row
of chart from right to left. Strand yarn
not in use loosely across wrong side to
keep fabric elastic.

# CHILD'S FAIR ISLE YOKED SWEATER

-◦❖◦-

## MAIN PART

WORKED IN ONE PIECE TO ARMHOLES

With 3mm (No 11/US 3) circular needle and
M, cast on 172(184:196) sts.
Mark end of cast on row to denote end of
rounds. Taking care not to twist the work, cont
in rounds of K1, P1 rib for 6cm/2¼in.
Change to 3¾mm (No 9/US 5) circular needle.
Work in rounds of st st (every round K) until
work measures 26(29:32)cm/10¼(11½:12½)in
from beg.

### Divide work as follows

**Next row** K80(85:90), turn.
**Next row** P74 (78:82), turn.
**Work backwards and forwards on this set of
sts only for Back.
**Next row** K1, K2 tog, K to last 3 sts, sl 1,
K1, psso, K1.
**Next row** P.
**Next row** K.
**Next row** P.
Rep last 4 rows twice more. 68(72:76) sts. **
Cont in st st without shaping until work
measures 32(36:40)cm/12½(14:15¾)in from
beg, ending with a P row. Leave these sts on a
spare needle.
With right side facing, slip next 12(14:16) sts
onto a safety pin, rejoin yarn to rem sts and
K74(78.82), turn; leaving rem 12(14:16) sts on
a safety pin.
Work on this set of sts only for Front. P 1 row.
Now work as given for Back from ** to **.
Cont in st st without shaping for a few rows
until work measures 30(34:38)cm/11¾(13¼:
15)in from beg, ending with a P row. Leave
these sts on a spare needle.

## LEFT SLEEVE

With set of four 3mm (No 11/US 3) needles
and M, cast on 48(52:56) sts.
Mark end of cast on row. Taking care not to
twist the work, cont in rounds of K1, P1 rib
for 10cm/4in.
**Next round** Rib 3(7:3), inc in next st, [rib 3,
inc in next st] to end. 60(64:70) sts.

Change to set of four 3¾mm (No 9/US 5) needles. K2 rounds.

**Next round** K1, m1, K to last st, m1, K1.

**Next 5 rounds** K.

Rep last 6 rounds 7 times more. 76(80:86) sts. Cont in st st without shaping until work measures 35(38:41)cm/13¾(15:16)in from beg.

### Graft Sleeve

Now slip last 20(22:24) sts of last round and first 18(20:22) sts of next round onto one needle; leaving rem 38(38:40) sts on a length of yarn. With one of the set of four 3mm (No 11/US 2) needles and right side facing, pick up but do not K 14(15:16) sts down left back armhole edge, slip 12(14:16) sts from safety pin onto needle, then pick up and 12(13:14) sts up left front armhole edge.

Graft sleeve sts on needle with armhole sts (see diagram page 39).

### RIGHT SLEEVE

Work as given for Left Sleeve, reversing grafting.

### YOKE

With 3¾mm (No 9/US 5) circular needle, M and right side facing, K across 38(38:40) left sleeve sts, 68(72:76) front sts, 38(38:40) right sleeve sts and 68(72:76) back sts. 212(220:232) sts. Mark end of last round. Work in rounds of st st as follows:

K 1 round dec 8(4:4) sts evenly across. 204(216:228) sts.

**1st to 18th rounds** Work 1st to 18th rows of chart.

With A, K 1 round.

**Next round** With A, *K2(3:4), [K2 tog, K3] 20(21:22) times; rep from * once more. 164(174:184) sts.

**Next round** [1A, 1B] to end.

**Next round** [1B, 1A] to end.

With A, K 1 round.

**Next round** With A, *K6(3:0), [K2 tog, K2] 19(21:23) times; rep from * once more. 126(132:138) sts.

**Next round** [2A, 1M, 3A] to end.

**Next round** [1A, 1B, 1A, 1B, 2A] to end.

**Next round** [1C, 3M, 2C] to end.

**Next round** With M, [K3, K2 tog, K1] to end. 105(110:115) sts.

With M, K 2 rounds dec 3(4:5) sts evenly across last round. 102(106:110) sts.

Change to set of four 3mm (No 11/US 3) needles.

Work 6cm/2¼in in rounds of K1, P1 rib for neckband. Cast off loosely in rib.

### TO COMPLETE

Fold neckband in half to wrong side and slip stitch in place. Hand wash in lukewarm water. Pat dry in towel. Stretch out to size and shape and dry flat away from heat and sunlight.

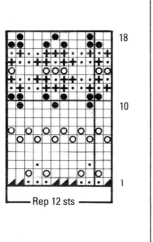

KEY

• Mist (M)
◢ Dusk
☐ White (A)
○ Twilight (B)
● Wild
   Violet
+ Pink

Rep 12 sts

## MATERIALS

3(3:4) 1oz hanks of Jamieson and Smith Shetland 2 ply Jumper Weight in Dark Brown (80) M.

2(3:3) 1oz hanks of same in each of Beige (FC43) A, Gold (28) and Rust (122).

1(2:2) 1oz hanks of same in each of Mid Brown (143) and Light Brown (120).

1×1oz hank in each of Orange (32), Olive (83) and Green (FC24).

One in each of 3mm (No 11/US 2) and 3¼mm (No 10/US 4) circular needles, 80cm long.

One set of four 3mm (No 11/US 2) double pointed knitting needles.

## MEASUREMENTS

To fit bust 81–87(91–97:102–107)cm
32–34(36–38:40–42)in
All round at bust 99(107:116)cm
39(42:45¾)in
Length to shoulder 67cm/26½in

## TENSION

29 sts and 29 rows to 10cm/4in square measured over patt on 3¼mm (No 10/US 4) needles.

## ABBREVIATIONS

See page 8.

## NOTE

The stitches shown on charts do not include stitches decreased when shaping armholes.

When working in patt from chart, read K rounds or rows from right to left and P rows from left to right.

Strand yarn not in use loosely across wrong side to keep fabric elastic.

# FAIR ISLE LONG LINE SLIPOVER

## MAIN PART
### WORKED IN ONE PIECE TO ARMHOLES

With 3mm (No 11/US 2) circular needle and M, cast on 240(260:280) sts. Mark end of cast on row to denote end of rounds. Taking care not to twist the work, cont in rounds as follows: K 1 round, P 1 round.

**Next round** [K1A, 1M] to end.

**Next 6 rounds** [P1A, A yarn back, K1M, A yarn forward] to end.

Now work welt patt from chart 1 as follows:

**1st round** Work last 10(4:0) sts of 1st row of chart 1, then rep 20 sts 11(12:14) times, work first 10(16:0) sts.

**2nd to 19th rounds** Rep 1st round 18 times, but working 2nd to 19th rows of chart 1.

Cont in rib across all sts until work measures 9cm/3½in from beg.

**Next round** With M, K5(4:5), m1, [K5, m1] to last 0(1:0) st, K0(1:0). 288(312:336) sts.

Change to 3¼mm (No 10/US 4) circular needle. Work in st st (every round K) and patt from charts as follows:

**★★1st round** Work last 12(5:0) sts of 1st row of chart 2, rep 24 sts 11(12:14) times, work first 12(19:0) sts.

**2nd to 7th rounds** Rep last round 6 times, but working 2nd to 7th rows of chart 2.

**Next round** Work last 12(5:0) sts of chart 3, rep 24 sts 11(12:14) times, work first 12(19:10) sts.

Cont working from chart 3 as set on last round until last row of chart 3 has been worked.

Rep from ★★ for patt but instead of chart 3, work charts 4, 5, 6, 7, 8 and 9 on subsequent repeats. Cont in patt until work measures 40cm/15¾in from beg.

### Divide work as follows

**Next row** Sl first 11(10:11) sts onto a safety pin, rejoin yarn to next st and patt 121(133:145) sts for Back, sl next 12(13:12) sts onto a safety pin, turn.

Work backwards and forwards on Back sts only.

Keeping patt correct, dec one st at each end of every row until 97(109:121) sts rem.

Cont without shaping until work measures 67cm/26½in from beg, ending with a wrong side row. Leave these sts on a spare needle.

With right side facing, sl next 11(10:11) sts onto a safety pin, rejoin yarn to rem sts, patt 121(133:145) sts for Front, sl last 12(13:12) sts onto a safety pin, turn. Work backwards and forwards on Front sts only.

Keeping patt correct, dec one st at each end of every row until 97(109:121) sts rem. Patt 1 row.

### Shape Neck

**Next row** Patt 48(54:60), turn. Work on this set of sts only.

Keeping patt correct, dec one st at neck edge on every alt row until 25(30:34) sts rem.

Cont without shaping until work measures same as Back, ending with a wrong side row. Leave these sts on a spare needle.

With right side facing, sl centre 1 st onto a safety pin, rejoin yarn to rem sts and patt to end. Complete to match first side.

### Join Shoulders

With right sides of Back and Front together, cast off together 25(30:34) shoulder sts (see diagram page 39), leaving centre 47(49:53) back neck sts on a holder.

### NECKBAND

With set of four 3mm (No 11/US 2) needles, M and right side facing, K across 47(49:53) back neck sts, pick up and K 62 sts down left front neck, K st from centre front, pick up and K 62 sts up right front neck. 172(174:178) sts. Mark end of last round. Work in rounds as follows:

**1st round** [K1A, 1M] to end.

**2nd round** [P1A, A yarn back, K1M, A yarn forward] to 3 sts before centre front st, P1A, A yarn back, with M, sl 1, K1, psso, K1, K2 tog, [A yarn forward, P1A, A yarn back, K1M] to end.

**3rd round** Rib to 1 st before centre front st, K3M, rib to end.

Cont in rib as set, dec one st at each side of centre front st on next and 2 foll alt rounds.

With M, K 1 round, dec at each side of centre front st as before. Cast off purlwise dec as before.

## ARMBANDS

With set of four 3 mm (No 11/US 2) needles, M and right side facing, rejoin yarn to 11(10:11) sts on 2nd safety pin at one armhole, K across these sts, pick up and K133 sts evenly around armhole edge, then K 12(13:12) sts from first safety pin. 156 sts.

**Next round** [K1A, 1M] to end.

**Next 8 rounds** [P1A, A yarn back, K1M, A yarn forward] to end.

With M, K 1 round. Cast off purlwise.

## TO COMPLETE

Wash in lukewarm water. Pat dry in towel. Stretch out to size and shape. Dry flat away from heat or sunlight.

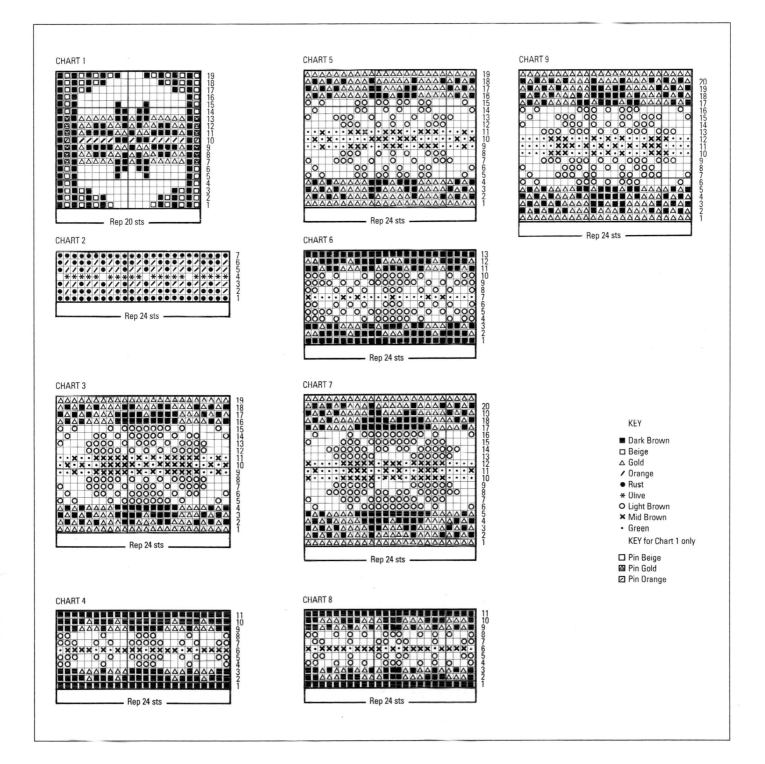

CHART 1
Rep 20 sts

CHART 2
Rep 24 sts

CHART 3
Rep 24 sts

CHART 4
Rep 24 sts

CHART 5
Rep 24 sts

CHART 6
Rep 24 sts

CHART 7
Rep 24 sts

CHART 8
Rep 24 sts

CHART 9
Rep 24 sts

KEY
■ Dark Brown
□ Beige
△ Gold
⁄ Orange
● Rust
✳ Olive
○ Light Brown
✕ Mid Brown
• Green
KEY for Chart 1 only
□ Pin Beige
▨ Pin Gold
▨ Pin Orange

## MATERIALS

3×2oz hanks of Jamieson and Smith Shetland 2 ply Jumper Weight in Shetland Black (5) M.
1×2oz hank of same in each of Light Brown (4) A, Natural (202), Light Grey (203) and Dark Fawn (78) B.
2×1oz hanks of same in each of Mid Grey (27) and Dark Grey (54) C.
1×1oz hank of same in White (1).
One in each of 2¾mm (No 12/US 2) and 3¼mm (No 10/US 4) circular needles, 80cm long.
One set of four in each of 2¾mm (No 12/US 2) and 3¼mm (No 10/US 4) double pointed knitting needles.

## MEASUREMENTS

To fit bust or chest
81-87(91-97:102-107)cm
32-34(36-38:40-42)in
All round at bust or chest
99(108:116)cm/39(42½:45½)in
Length to shoulder 65(67:69)cm
25½(26½:27¼)in
Sleeve length 52(55:55)cm
20½(21½:21½)in

## TENSION

29 sts and 29 rows to 10cm/4in square measured over patt on 3¼mm (No 10/US 4) needles.

## ABBREVIATIONS

See page 8.

## NOTE

The stitches shown on charts do not include stitches decreased when shaping armholes or sleeves.
When working in patt from chart, read K rounds or rows from right to left and P rows from left to right.
Strand yarn not in use loosely across wrong side to keep fabric elastic.

# FAIR ISLE SWEATER IN NATURAL SHADES

## MAIN PART

WORKED IN ONE PIECE TO ARMHOLES

With 2¾mm (No 12/US 2) circular needle and M, cast on 224(248:268) sts.
Mark end of cast on row to denote end of rounds. Taking care not to twist the work, cont in rounds as follows: Work 1 round in K2, P2 rib.
**1st to 4th rounds** [K2A, M yarn forward, P2M, M yarn back] to end.
**5th to 8th rounds** [K2C, M yarn forward, P2M, M yarn back] to end.
**9th to 12th rounds** [K2B, M yarn forward, P2M, M yarn back] to end.
**13th to 16th rounds** As 5th to 8th rounds.
**17th to 20th rounds** As 1st to 4th rounds. **
**Next round** *With M, [K2 (3:3), inc in next st, K3, inc in next st] 16(14:16) times, [K2, inc in next st] 0(4:2) times; rep from * once more. 288(312:336) sts.
Change to 3¼mm (No 10/US 4) circular needle and K1 round in M.
Work in rounds of st st (every round K) and patt from charts as follows:
**1st to 7th rounds** Work 17th to 23rd rows of chart 2, dec one st at centre and end (side seams) of last round on 1st size and inc one st at centre and end (side seams) of last round on 3rd size. 286(312:338) sts.
**8th round** Work last 6(0:6) sts of 1st row of chart 1, rep 26 sts 10(12:12) times, work first 20(0:20) sts.
**9th to 22nd rounds** Rep last round 14 times, but working 2nd to 15th rows of chart 1.
**23rd to 45th rounds** Inc one st at each seam of 1st round on 1st size and dec one st at each seam of 1st round on 3rd size, work 1st to 23rd rows of chart 3, dec one st at each seam on last round on 1st size and inc one st at each seam on last round on 3rd size.
**46th round** Work last 6(0:6) sts of 1st row of chart 4, rep 26 sts 10(12:12) times, work first 20(0:20) sts
**47th to 56th rounds** Rep last round 10 times, but working 2nd to 11th rows of chart 4.

**57th to 72nd rounds** Inc one st at each seam of 1st round on 1st size and dec one st at each seam of 1st round on 3rd size, work 1st to 16th rows of chart 2.

These 72 rounds form patt. Cont in patt, working appropriate repeats of chart 1 and chart 4 until work measures 42(43:44)cm/16½(17: 17¼)in from beg, ending with a 36th(38th:42nd) round of patt.

### Divide work as follows

★★★**Next row** Patt 11 and slip these sts onto a safety pin, patt 122(134:146) sts for Front, slip next 11 sts onto a safety pin, turn.

Work backwards and forwards on Front sts only.

**Next row** Patt to end.

**Next row** Patt 1, K2 tog tbl, patt to last 3 sts, K2 tog, patt 1.

Rep last 2 rows 3 times more. 114(126:138) sts.★★★

Keeping patt correct, cont without shaping until work measures 58(60:62)cm/22¾(23¾: 24½)in from beg, ending with a wrong side row.

### Shape Neck

**Next row** Patt 38(43:47), K2 tog, patt 1, turn. Work on this set of sts only.

**Next row** Patt to end.

**Next row** Patt to last 3 sts, K2 tog, patt 1.

Rep last 2 rows 7 times more. 32(37:41) sts.

Cont without shaping for a few rows until work measures 65(67:69)cm/25½(26½:27¼)in from beg, ending with a wrong side row. Leave these sts on a spare needle.

With right side facing, slip 32(34:38) centre Front sts onto a holder, rejoin yarn to rem sts, patt 1, K2 tog tbl, patt to end.

**Next row** Patt to end.

**Next row** Patt 1, K2 tog tbl, patt to end.

Complete to match first side of neck.

With right side facing, rejoin yarn to rem sts for Back and work as given for Front from ★★★ to ★★★.

Keeping patt correct, cont without shaping until work measures same as Front to shoulders, ending with a wrong side row.

### Join Shoulders

With right sides of Front and Back together, cast off together 32(37:41) shoulder sts as shown on diagram, leaving centre 50(52:56) back neck sts on a holder.

## SLEEVES

With set of four 3¼mm (No 10/US 4) needles, M and right side facing, slip 11 sts from 2nd safety pin at one armhole onto needle, pick up and K109(115:121) sts evenly around armhole edge, K11 sts from first safety pin. 131(137:143) sts. Mark end of last round. K1 round.

Work in rounds of st st and patt from charts as follows:

**1st round** Work last 3(6:3) sts of 7th(14th:14th) row of chart 2, then rep 12 sts to last 8(11:8) sts, work first 8(11:8) sts.

**2nd to 7th(14th:14th) rounds** Rep last round 6(13:13) times, but working chart 2 in reverse order from 6th(13th:13th) to 1st rows.

**Next round** Work last 0(3:6) sts of 11th row of chart 4 (2nd repeat), then rep 26 sts to last 1(4:7) sts, work first 1(4:7) sts.

Rep last round 10 times more, but working chart 4 in reverse order from 10th to 1st rows.

The last 11 rounds set patt. Cont in patt as set, matching to Main Part and working charts in reverse order, **at the same time**, dec one st at each end of 13th(11th:7th) round and every foll 4th round until 79(83:87) sts rem. Patt 2 rounds.

**Next round** With M, ★K0(1:2), [K2 tog, K2] 4 times; rep from ★ 3 times more, [K2 tog, K3] 3 times. 60(64:68) sts.

Change to set of four 2¾mm (No 12/US 2) needles.

Work as given for Main Part from ★★ to ★★. With M, rib 1 round. Cast off in rib.

## NECKBAND

With set of four 2¾mm (No 12/US 2) needles, M and right side facing, pick up and K20 sts down left front neck, K across 32(34:38) sts at centre front dec 4 sts evenly, pick up and K20 sts up right front neck and K across 50(52:56) sts on back neck dec 6 sts evenly. 112(116:124) sts.

Work 9th to 20th rounds of rib as given for Main Part. With M, rib 1 round. Cast off in rib.

## TO COMPLETE

Hand wash in lukewarm water. Pat dry in towel. Stretch out to size and shape. Dry flat away from heat or sunlight.

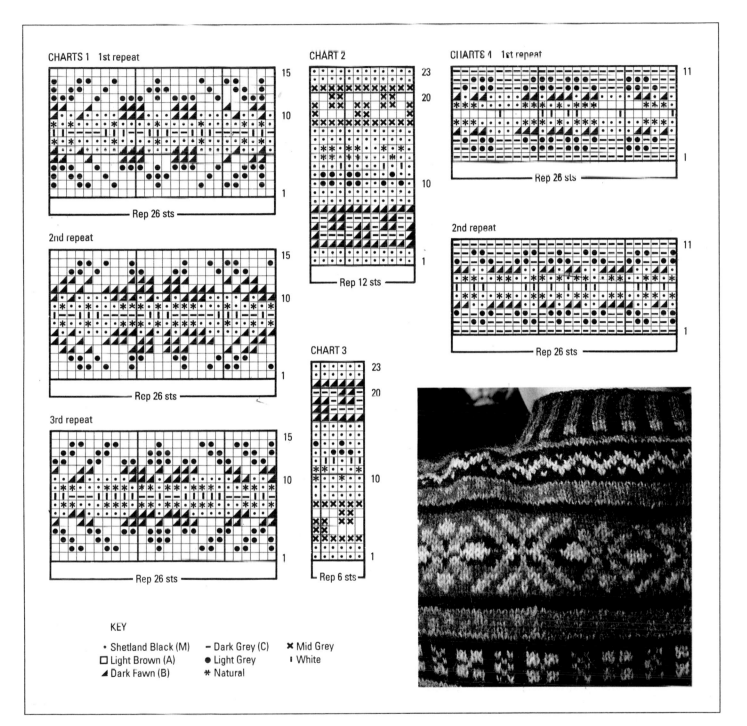

CHARTS 1   1st repeat

15
10
1

Rep 26 sts

2nd repeat

15
10
1

Rep 26 sts

3rd repeat

15
10
1

Rep 26 sts

CHART 2

23
20
10
1

Rep 12 sts

CHART 3

23
20
15
10
1

Rep 6 sts

CHARTS 4   1st repeat

11
1

Rep 26 sts

2nd repeat

11
1

Rep 26 sts

KEY

- Shetland Black (M)     – Dark Grey (C)     ✕ Mid Grey
- □ Light Brown (A)        ● Light Grey          ı White
- ▲ Dark Fawn (B)         ✱ Natural

## MATERIALS

10(11) 100g balls of Wendy Guernsey 5
ply.
One pair of 3mm (No 11/US 3)
knitting needles.
Cable needle.

## MEASUREMENTS

To fit bust 86–97(102–112)cm
34–38(40–44)in
All round at bust 122(137)cm/48(54)in
Length to shoulder 70(74)cm
27½(29)in
Sleeve seam 43(47)cm/17(18½)in

## TENSION

28 sts and 36 rows to 10cm/4in square
measured over st st on 3mm (No 11/
US 3) needles.

## ABBREVIATIONS

See page 8.

# TREE OF
LIFE
GANSEY

### PANEL A
WORKED OVER 12 STS

**1st row (right side)** P2, K8, P2.
**2nd row** K2, P8, K2.
**3rd and 4th rows** Work 1st and 2nd rows.
**5th row** P2, sl next 4 sts onto cable needle and
leave at back, K4, then K4 from cable needle,
P2.
**6th row** As 2nd row.
**7th and 8th rows** Work 1st and 2nd rows.
These 8 rows form patt.

### PANEL B
WORKED OVER 9 STS

**1st row (right side)** P1, K8.
**2nd row** P7, K2.
**3rd row** P3, K6.
**4th row** P5, K4.
**5th row** P5, K4.
*6th row* P3, K6.
**7th row** P7, K2.
**8th row** P1, K8.
**9th row** P9.
**10th row** As 8th row.
**11th row** As 7th row.
**12th row** As 6th row.
**13th row** As 5th row.
**14th row** As 4th row.
**15th row** As 3rd row.
**16th row** As 2nd row.
These 16 rows form patt.

### PANEL C
WORKED OVER 21 STS

**1st row (right side)** K9, P1, K1, P1, K9.
**2nd row** P8, K2, P1, K2, P8.
**3rd row** K7, P2, K3, P2, K7.
**4th row** P6, K2, P5, K2, P6.
**5th row** K5, P2, K2, P1, K1, P1, K2, P2, K5.
**6th row** P4, K2, P2, K2, P1, K2, P2, K2, P4.
**7th row** K3, [P2, K2, P2, K3] twice.
**8th row** [P2, K2] twice, P5, [K2, P2] twice.
**9th row** K1, [P2, K2] twice, P1, K1, P1, [K2,
P2] twice, K1.
**10th row** P1, K1, [P2, K2] twice, P1, [K2, P2]
twice, K1, P1.

**11th row** As 7th row.
**12th row** As 8th row.
**13th row** K2, [P1, K2, P2, K2, P1, K1] twice, K1.
**14th row** As 6th row.
**15th row** As 7th row.
**16th row** P3, K1, P2, K2, P5, K2, P2, K1, P3.
**17th row** As 5th row.
**18th row** As 6th row.
**19th row** K4, P1, K2, P2, K3, P2, K2, P1, K4.
**20th row** As 4th row.
**21st row** As 5th row.
**22nd row** P5, K1, P2, K2, P1, K2, P2, K1, P5.
**23rd row** As 3rd row.
**24th row** As 4th row.
**25th row** K6, P1, K2, P1, K1, P1, K2, P1, K6.
**26th row** As 2nd row.
**27th row** As 3rd row.
**28th row** P7, K1, P5, K1, P7.
**29th row** As 3rd row.
**30th row** As 2nd row.
**31st row** As 1st row.
**32nd row** P21.
These 32 rows form patt.

### PANEL D
WORKED OVER 9 STS

**1st row (right side)** K8, P1.
**2nd row** K2, P7.
**3rd row** K6, P3.
**4th row** K4, P5.
**5th row** K4, P5.
**6th row** K6, P3.
**7th row** K2, P7.
**8th row** K8, P1.
**9th row** P9.
**10th row** As 8th row.
**11th row** As 7th row.
**12th row** As 6th row.
**13th row** As 5th row.
**14th row** As 4th row.
**15th row** As 3rd row.
**16th row** As 2nd row.
These 16 rows form patt.

### BACK

With 3mm (No 11/US 3) needles cast on 182(202) sts.
**1st row (right side)** K2, [P2, K2] to end.
**2nd row** P2, [K2, P2] to end.
Rep these 2 rows until work measures 6(8)cm/ 2¼(3)in from beg, ending with a 2nd row and inc one st at centre of last row. 183(203) sts.
Beg with a K row, cont in st st until work measures 11(15)cm/4¼(6)in from beg, ending with a P row.
Work in patt as follows:
**1st size only**
**1st row (right side)** K3, ★ work 1st row of Panel A, K2, work 1st row of Panel B, Panel C and Panel D, K2; rep from ★ to last 15 sts, work 1st row of Panel A, K3.
**2nd row** P3, ★ work 2nd row of Panel A, P2, work 2nd row of Panel D, Panel C and Panel B, P2; rep from ★ to last 15 sts, work 2nd row of Panel A, P3.
**2nd size only**
**1st row (right side)** K2, work 1st row of Panel D, K2, ★ work 1st row of Panel A, K2, work 1st row of Panel B, Panel C and Panel D, K2; rep from ★ to last 25 sts, work 1st row of Panel A, K2, work 1st row of Panel B, K2.
**2nd row** P2, work 2nd row of Panel B, P2, ★ work 2nd row of Panel A, P2, work 2nd row of Panel D, Panel C and Panel B, P2; rep from ★ to last 25 sts, work 2nd row of Panel A, P2, work 2nd row of Panel D, P2.
**All sizes**
These 2 rows set patt. Cont in patt, working appropriate rows of Panels until work measures approximately 68(72)cm/26¾(28¼)in from beg, ending with a 26th row of Panel C.

#### *Shape Neck*
**Next row** Patt 70(80), turn. Work on this set of sts only.
Cast off 4 sts at beg of next row and 3 sts at beg of 2 foll alt rows. Cast off rem 60(70) sts. With right side facing, sl centre 43 sts onto a holder, rejoin yarn to rem sts and patt 2 rows. Complete as given for first side.

### FRONT

Work as given for Back until work measures approximately 61(65)cm/24(25½)in from beg, ending with a 32nd row of Panel C.

#### *Shape Neck*
**Next row** Patt 81(91), turn. Work on this set of sts only.
Keeping patt correct, cast off 6 sts at beg of next row, 4 sts at beg of 3 foll alt rows and 3 sts at beg of next alt row. 60(70) sts.

Patt 22 rows straight. Cast off.

With right side facing, sl centre 21 sts onto a holder, rejoin yarn to rem sts and patt 2 rows. Complete as given for first side.

### SLEEVES

With 3mm (No 11/US 3) needles cast on 74(78) sts. Work 6cm/2¼in in rib as given for Back, ending with a 1st row.

**Next row** Rib 1(3), m1, [rib 8, m1] to last 1(3) sts, rib 1(3). 84(88) sts.

Beg with a K row, cont in st st and inc one st at each end of 1st and every alt row until there are 128(148) sts, ending with a P row.

Now work in patt as given for Back until work measures approximately 43(47)cm/17(18½)in from beg, ending with a 32nd row of Panel C. Cast off.

### NECKBAND

Join right shoulder seam.

With 3mm (No 11/US 3) needles and right side facing, pick up and K 37 sts down left front neck, K across 21 sts at centre front dec one st, pick up and K 37 sts up right front neck, 9 sts down right back neck, K across 43 sts at back neck dec 5 sts evenly, pick up and K 9 sts up left back neck. 150 sts. Beg with a 2nd row, work in rib as given for Back for 8cm/3in. Cast off in rib.

### TO MAKE UP

Join left shoulder and neckband seam. Fold neckband in half to wrong side and slip stitch in position. Sew on sleeves, placing centre of sleeves to shoulder seams. Join side and sleeve seams.

## MATERIALS

9(10) 100g balls of Wilkinsons Guernsey
5 ply.
1 pair in each of 2¼mm (No 13/US 2)
and 3mm (No 11/US 4) knitting
needles.
Cable needle.

## MEASUREMENTS

To fit bust 81–91(97–107)cm
32–36(38–42)in
All round at bust 108(122)cm
42½(48)in
Length to shoulder 67(70)cm
26½(27½)in
Sleeve seam 44(47)cm/17¼(18½)in

## TENSION

26 sts and 38 rows to 10cm/4in square
measured over st st on 3mm (No 11/
US 4) needles.

## ABBREVIATIONS

See page 8.

# GANSEY STYLE SWEATER

---◈---

## PANEL A
WORKED OVER 8(10) STS

**1st row (right side)** P2(3), K4, P2(3).
**2nd row** K2(3), P4, K2(3).
**3rd row** P2(3), sl next 2 sts onto cable needle
and leave at back, K2, then K2 from cable
needle, P2(3).
**4th row** As 2nd row.
These 4 rows form patt.

## PANEL B
WORKED OVER 19 STS

**1st row (right side)** K7, P2, K1, P2, K7.
**2nd row** P6, K2, P3, K2, P6.
**3rd row** K5, [P2, K5] twice.
**4th row** P4, K2, P2, K1, P1, K1, P2, K2, P4.
**5th row** K3, P2, K2, P2, K1, P2, K2, P2, K3.
**6th row** [P2, K2] twice, P3, [K2, P2] twice.
**7th row** K1, P2, K2, P2, K5, P2, K2, P2, K1.
**8th row** P1, [K1, P2, K2, P2, K1, P1] twice.
**9th row** As 5th row.
**10th row** As 6th row.
**11th row** K2, P1, K2, P2, K5, P2, K2, P1, K2.
**12th row** As 4th row.
**13th row** As 5th row.
**14th row** P3, K1, P2, K2, P3, K2, P2, K1, P3.
**15th row** As 3rd row.
**16th row** As 4th row.
**17th row** K4, P1, K2, P2, K1, P2, K2, P1, K4.
**18th row** As 2nd row.
**19th row** K6, P1, K5, P1, K6.
**20th row** P8, K1, P1, K1, P8.
**21st row** As 1st row.
**22nd row** P7, K1, P3, K1, P7.
**23rd row** K8, P1, K1, P1, K8.
**24th row** As 20th row.
**25th row** K19.
**26th row** P19.
These 26 rows form patt.

## BACK

With 2¼mm (No 13/US 2) needles cast on
134(150) sts.
**1st row (right side)** K2, [P2, K2] to end.
**2nd row** P2, [K2, P2] to end.
Rep these 2 rows until work measures 8cm/3in
from beg, ending with a 2nd row and inc 13(15)

sts evenly across last row. 147(165) sts.
Change to 3mm (No 11/US 4) needles. Work bodice in patt as follows:

**1st row (right side)** K1(2), P1, ★ K7, P1; rep from ★ to last 1(2) sts, K1(2).

**2nd row** P0(1), K1, P1, K1, ★ P5, K1, P1, K1; rep from ★ to last 0(1) st, P0(1).

**3rd row** K1(2), P1, ★ K5, [P1, K1] 3 times, K4, P1; rep from ★ to last 1(2) sts, K1(2).

**4th row** P0(1), K1, P1, K1, ★ P3, [K1, P1] 4 times, P2, K1, P1, K1; rep from ★ to last 0(1) st, P0(1).

**5th row** K1(2), P1, ★ K3, [P1, K1] 5 times, K2, P1; rep from ★ to last 1(2) sts, K1(2).

**6th row** P0(1), K1, ★ P1, K1; rep from ★ to last 0(1) st, P0(1).

**7th row** As 5th row.

**8th row** As 4th row.

**9th row** As 3rd row.

**10th row** As 2nd row.

**11th row** As 1st row.

**12th row** P0(1), K1, P1, K1, ★ P13, K1, P1, K1; rep from ★ to last 0(1) st, P0(1).

These 12 rows form bodice patt. Cont in bodice patt until work measures 38(41)cm/15(16)in from beg, ending with a 12th row of patt and dec 6 sts evenly across last row. 141(159) sts. Work border patt as follows:

**1st to 4th rows** P.

**5th row (right side)** K4, ★ P1, K5; rep from ★ to last 5 sts, P1, K4.

**6th row** P3, ★ K1, P1, K1, P3; rep from ★ to end.

**7th row** P1, K1, P1, ★ K3, P1, K1, P1; rep from ★ to end.

**8th row** P1, K1, ★ P5, K1; rep from ★ to last st, P1.

**9th row** As 7th row.

**10th row** As 6th row.

**11th row** As 5th row.

**12th to 15th rows** P.

**16th row** P 8(12), P twice in each of next 2 sts, P23(25), ★ P twice in each of next 2 sts, P10(11), P twice in next st, P11(12), P twice in each of next 2 sts, P23(25); rep from ★ once more, P twice in each of next 2 sts, P8(12). 155(173) sts. Work in yoke patt as follows:

**1st row (right side)** K6(9), work 1st row of Panel A, ★ work 1st row of Panel B, then Panel A; rep from ★ to last 6(9) sts, K6(9).

**2nd row** K6(9), work 2nd row of Panel A, ★ work 2nd row of Panel B, then Panel A; rep from ★ to last 6(9) sts, K6(9).

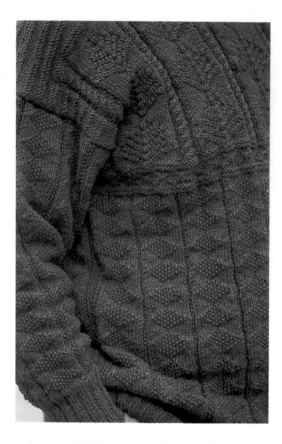

**3rd row** K6(9), work 3rd row of Panel A, ★ work 3rd row of Panel B, then Panel A; rep from ★ to last 6(9) sts, K6(9).

**4th row** P6(9), work 4th row of Panel A, ★ work 4th row of Panel B, then Panel A; rep from ★ to last 6(9) sts, P6(9).

**5th row** K6(9), work 1st row of Panel A, ★ work 5th row of Panel B, work 1st row of Panel A; rep from ★ to last 6(9) sts, K6(9).

**6th row** P6(9), work 2nd row of Panel A, ★ work 6th row of Panel B, work 2nd row of Panel A; rep from ★ to last 6(9) sts, P6(9).

These 6 rows set yoke patt. Cont in yoke patt working appropriate rows of Panels until 78 rows of yoke patt in all have been worked.
★★ Change to 2¼mm (No 13/US 0) needles. K 5 rows. P 1 row. K 1 row. P 1 row.
Rep last 8 rows until work measures 67(70)cm/26½(27½)in from beg, ending with a wrong side row.★★

### Shape Shoulders

Cast off 26(29) sts at beg of next 4 rows. Leave rem 51(57) sts on a holder.

## FRONT

Work as given for Back until 64 rows of yoke patt in all have been worked.

### Shape Neck

**Next row** Patt 64(71), turn. Work on this set of sts only.
Keeping patt correct, dec one st at neck edge on every row until 52(58) sts rem. Patt 1(0) rows.
Now work as given for Back from ★★ to ★★.

### Shape Shoulder

Cast off 26(29) sts at beg of next row. Work 1 row. Cast off rem 26(29) sts.
With right side facing, sl centre 27(31) sts onto a holder, rejoin yarn to rem sts, patt to end. Complete to match first side, reversing shoulder shaping.

## SLEEVES

With 2¼mm (No 13/US 2) needles cast on 58(66) sts. Work in rib as given for Back for 8cm/3in, ending with a 1st row.
**Next row** Rib 5(1), [inc in next st, rib 1(3) sts] to last 5(1) sts, inc in next st, rib 4(0). 83 sts.
Change to 3mm (No 11/US 4) needles.
Work in bodice patt as given for 1st size on Back, **at the same time**, inc one st at each end of 5th and 13 foll 4th rows, then on every foll 5th row until there are 135(141) sts, working inc sts into bodice patt.
Cont without shaping until work measures 44(47)cm/17¼(18½)in from beg, ending with a 12th row of patt. Cast off.

## NECKBAND

Join right shoulder seam.
With 2¼mm (No 13/US 2) needles and right side facing, pick up and K 29 sts down left front neck, K across 27(31) centre front sts dec 2(3) sts evenly, pick up and K 29 sts up right front neck and K across 51(57) back neck sts dec 4(5) sts evenly. 130(138) sts.
Beg with a 2nd row, work in rib as given for Back for 4cm/1½in, ending with a 2nd row. K 6 rows. Cast off knitwise.

## TO MAKE UP

Join left shoulder and neckband seam. Sew on sleeves, placing centre of sleeves to shoulder seams. Join side and sleeve seams.

## MATERIALS

15(17) 50g balls of Hayfield Pure Wool
Classics DK.
1 pair in each of 3mm (No 11/US 3)
and 3¾mm (No 9/US 5) knitting
needles.
Cable needle.

## MEASUREMENTS

To fit chest 97-102(107-112)cm
38-40(42-44)in
All round at chest 115(126)cm
45¼(49½)in
Length to shoulder 67(69)cm
26½(27)in
Sleeve seam 51cm/20in

## TENSION

23 sts and 29 rows to 10cm/4in square
measured over st st on 3¾mm (No 9/
US 5) needles.

## ABBREVIATIONS

C4B-sl next 2 sts onto cable needle and
leave at back, K2, then K2 from cable
needle.
C4F-sl next 2 sts onto cable needle and
leave at front, K2, then K2 from cable
needle.
Tw2-K2 tog, do not drop sts off left-
hand needle, K first st again, slipping
both sts off needle.
Also see page 8.

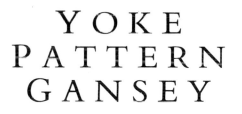

# YOKE PATTERN GANSEY

### PANEL A
WORKED OVER 15 STS

**1st row (right side)** K7, P1, K7.
**2nd row** P6, K1, P1, K1, P6.
**3rd row** K5, P1, [K1, P1] twice, K5.
**4th row** P4, K1, [P1, K1] 3 times, P4.
**5th row** K3, P1, [K1, P1] 4 times, K3.
**6th row** P2, K1, [P1, K1] 5 times, P2.
**7th row** As 5th row.
**8th row** As 4th row.
**9th row** As 3rd row.
**10th row** As 2nd row.
**11th row** As 1st row.
**12th row** P15.
These 12 rows form patt.

### PANEL B
WORKED OVER 19 STS

**1st row (right side)** K8, P1, K1, P1, K8.
**2nd row** P19.
**3rd row** As 1st row.
**4th row** P7, K1, P3, K1, P7.
**5th row** K6, P1, K5, P1, K6.
**6th row** P5, K1, P2, K1, P1, K1, P2, K1, P5.
**7th row** K4, P1, K2, P1, K3, P1, K2, P1, K4.
**8th row** P3, K1, P2, K1, P5, K1, P2, K1, P3.
**9th row** [K2, P1] 3 times, K1, [P1, K2] 3 times.
**10th row** P4, K1, P2, K1, P3, K1, P2, K1, P4.
**11th row** K3, P1, K2, P1, K5, P1, K2, P1, K3.
**12th row** As 6th row.
**13th row** As 7th row.
**14th row** P6, K1, P5, K1, P6.
**15th row** K5, P1, K2, P1, K1, P1, K2, P1, K5.
**16th row** As 4th row.
**17th row** As 5th row.
**18th row** P8, K1, P1, K1, P8.
**19th row** K7, P1, K3, P1, K7.
**20th row** P19.
**21st row** As 1st row.
**22nd row** P19.
**23rd row** K9, P1, K9.
**24th row** P19.
These 24 rows form patt.

### BACK

With 3mm (No 11/US 3) needles cast on
133(145) sts.
Work in rib patt as follows:

**1st row (right side)** K1 tbl, [P1, K1 tbl] to end.

**2nd row** P1, [K1 tbl, P1] to end.

Rep these 2 rows until work measures 7cm/2¾in from beg, ending with a wrong side row.

Change to 3¾mm (No 9/US 5) needles.

Beg with a K row, cont in st st until work measures 42(43)cm/16½(17)in from beg, ending with a K row.

Work border patt as follows:

**1st row (wrong side)** K.

**2nd and 3rd rows** P.

**4th row** K.

**5th row** P3, [K1, P5] to last 4 sts, K1, P3.

**6th row** K2, [P1, K1, P1, K3] to last 5 sts, P1, K1, P1, K2.

**7th row** P1, [K1, P3, K1, P1] to end.

**8th row** P1, [K5, P1] to end.

**9th row** As 7th row.

**10th row** As 6th row.

**11th row** As 5th row.

**12th row** K.

**13th and 14th rows** P.

**15th and 16th rows** K.

**Next row** P49(55), P twice in each of next 2 sts, P31, P twice in each of next 2 sts, P49(55). 137(149) sts.

Work yoke patt as follows:

**1st row (right side)** K1, [P1, K1] 2(5) times, ★ P2, Tw2, P2, work 1st row of Panel A, P2, Tw2, P2 ★; K1, [P1, K1] 5 times, P2, Tw2, P2, K4, P2, Tw2, P2, work 1st row of Panel B, P2, Tw2, P2, K4, P2, Tw2, P2, K1, [P1, K1] 5 times, rep from ★ to ★ once, K1, [P1, K1] 2(5) times.

**2nd row** K1, [P1, K1] 2(5) times, ★ K2, P2, K2, work 2nd row of Panel A, K2, P2, K2 ★; K13, P2, K2, P4, K2, P2, K2, work 2nd row of Panel B, K2, P2, K2, P4, K2, P2, K13, rep from ★ to ★ once, K1, [P1, K1] 2(5) times.

**3rd row** K1, [P1, K1] 2(5) times, ★ P2, Tw2, P2, work 3rd row of Panel A, P2, Tw2, P2 ★; K1, [P1, K1] 5 times, P2, Tw2, P2, C4B, P2, Tw2, P2, work 3rd row of Panel B, P2, Tw2, P2, C4F, P2, Tw2, P2, K1, [P1, K1] 5 times, rep from ★ to ★ once, K1, [P1, K1] 2(5) times.

**4th row** K1, [P1, K1] 2(5) times, ★ K2, P2, K2, work 4th row of Panel A, K2, P2, K2 ★; K13, P2, K2, P4, K2, P2, K2, work 4th row of Panel B, K2, P2, K2, P4, K2, P2, K13, rep from ★ to ★ once, K1, [P1, K1] 2(5) times.

These 4 rows set yoke patt. Cont in yoke patt,

working appropriate rows of Panels, work a further 44 rows. K 1 row. P 2 rows. K 2 rows. P 1 row.

Now work as follows:

**1st row (right side)** K1, [P1, K1] to end.
**2nd row** K.

Rep these 2 rows until work measures 67(69)cm/26½(27)in from beg, ending with a wrong side row.

### Shape Shoulders

Cast off 14(15) sts at beg of next 6 rows. Leave rem 53(59) sts on a holder.

### FRONT

Work as given for Back until Front is 14 rows less than Back to shoulder shaping, ending with a wrong side row.

### Shape Neck

**Next row** Patt 50(54), turn. Work on this set of sts only.

Keeping patt correct, dec one st at neck edge on every row until 42 (45) sts rem.

Patt 5(4) rows straight.

### Shape Shoulder

Cast off 14(15) sts at beg of next and foll alt row. Patt 1 row. Cast off rem 14(15) sts.

With right side facing, sl centre 37(41) sts onto a holder, rejoin yarn to rem sts and patt to end. Patt 1 row. Complete to match first side.

### SLEEVES

With 3mm (No 11/US 3) needles cast on 61(65) sts. Work in rib as given for Back for 7cm/2¾in, ending with a wrong side row and inc 6 sts evenly across last row. 67(71) sts.

Change to 3¾mm (No 9/US 5) needles.

Beg with a K row, work in st st and inc one st at each end of 3rd and 3(5) foll alt rows, then on every foll 4th row until there are 109(115) sts, ending with a K row.

Now work the 16 rows of border patt as given for Back, **at the same time**, inc one st at each end of 3 foll 5th rows, working inc sts into patt. 115(121) sts.

**Next row** P40(43), P twice in each of next 2 sts, P31, P twice in each of next 2 sts, P40(43). 119(125) sts.

Work in patt as follows:

**1st row (right side)** P2(1), [Tw2, P2] 0(1)

time, work 1st row of Panel A, ★ P2, Tw2, P2, K1, [P1, K1] 5 times, P2, Tw2, P2 ★; K4, P2, Tw2, P2, work 1st row of Panel B, P2, Tw2, P2, K4, rep from ★ to ★ once, work 1st row of Panel A, [P2, Tw2] 0(1) time, P2(1).

**2nd row** K2(1), [P2, K2] 0(1) time, work 2nd row of Panel A, ★ K2, P2, K15, P2, K2 ★; P4, K2, P2, K2, work 2nd row of Panel B, K2, P2, K2, P4, rep from ★ to ★ once, work 2nd row of Panel A, [K2, P2] 0(1) time, K2(1).

**3rd row** P2(1), [Tw2, P2] 0(1) time, work 3rd row of Panel A, ★ P2, Tw2, P2, K1, [P1, K1] 5 times, P2, Tw2, P2 ★; C4B, P2, Tw2, P2, work 3rd row of Panel B, P2, Tw2, P2, C4F, rep from ★ to ★ once, work 3rd row of Panel A, [P2, Tw2] 0(1) time, P2(1).

**4th row** K2(1), [P2, K2] 0(1) time, work 4th row of Panel A, ★ K2, P2, K15, P2, K2 ★; P4, K2, P2, K2, work 4th row of Panel B, K2, P2, K2, P4, rep from ★ to ★ once, work 4th row of Panel A, [K2, P2] 0(1) time, K2(1).

These 4 rows set patt. Cont in patt as set, working appropriate rows of Panels, work a further 20 rows. K 1 row. P 2 rows. K 2 rows. P 1 row.

Now work as follows:

**1st row (right side)** K1, [P1, K1] to end.
**2nd row** K.

Rep these 2 rows until work measures 51cm/20in from beg, ending with a wrong side row. Cast off.

### NECKBAND

Join right shoulder seam.

With 3mm (No 11/US 3) needles and right side facing, pick up and K15 sts down left front neck, K1, [P1, K1] 18(20) times across centre front neck sts, pick up and K 15(16) sts up right front neck and K1(0), [P1, K1] 25(29) times P1 across back neck sts inc one st in last st on 1st size only. 121(131) sts. Beg with a 1st row, work 6 rows in rib as given for Back. K1 row for fold line. Rib 6 rows. Cast off loosely in rib.

### TO MAKE UP

Join left shoulder and neckband seam. Fold neckband at fold line to wrong side and slip stitch in position. Sew on sleeves, placing centre of sleeves to shoulder seams. Join side and sleeve seams.

## MATERIALS

9(10:11) 100g balls of Wendy Guernsey
5 ply.
One in each of 2¾mm (No 12/US 2)
and 3mm (No 11/US 3) circular
needles, 80cm long.
Set of four in each of 2¾mm (No 12/
US 2) and 3mm (No 11/US 3) double
pointed knitting needles.
Cable needle.
3 buttons.

## MEASUREMENTS

To fit bust 81-87(91-97:102-107)cm
32-34(36-38:40-42)in
All round at bust 106(116:126)cm
41¾(45¾:49½)in
Length to shoulder 69(70:72)cm
27(27½:28¼)in
Sleeve seam 43cm/17in

## TENSION

28 sts and 38 rows to 10cm/4in square
measured over bodice patt on 3mm
(No 11/US 3) needles.

## ABBREVIATIONS

C8–sl next 2 sts onto cable needle and
leave at back, K2, then K2 from cable
needle, sl next 2 sts onto cable needle
and leave at front, K2, then K2 from
cable needle.
C6–sl next 3 sts onto cable needle and
leave at back, K3, then K3 from cable
needle.
Tw2L–K into the back of 2nd st, then
K first st, slipping both sts off needle
together.
Tw2R–K into the front of 2nd st, then
K first st, slipping both sts off needle
together.
Also see page 8.

# 'SAMPLER' STYLE GANSEY

--◆--

## PANEL A

WORKED OVER 17(19:19) STS

**1st row (right side)** K 17(19:19).
**2nd row** P 17(19:19).
**3rd and 4th rows** As 1st and 2nd rows.
**5th row** K8(9:9), P1, K8(9:9).
**6th row and 14 foll alt rows** K the K sts, P
the P sts as they appear.
**7th row** K7(8:8), P1, K1, P1, K7(8:8).
**9th row** K6(7:7), P1, [K1, P1] twice, K6(7:7).
**11th row**: K5(6:6), P1, [K1, P1] 3 times,
K5(6:6).
**13th row** K4(5:5), P1, K1, P1, K3, P1, K1, P1,
K4(5:5).
**15th row** K3(4:4), P1, K1, P1, K5, P1, K1, P1,
K3(4:4).
**17th row** K2(3:3), P1, K1, P1, K7, P1, K1, P1,
K2(3:3).
**19th row** K1(2:2), P1, K1, P1, K9, P1, K1, P1,
K1(2:2).
**21st row** As 17th row.
**23rd row** As 15th row.
**25th row** As 13th row.
**27th row** As 11th row.
**29th row** As 9th row.
**31st row** As 7th row.
**33rd row** As 5th row.
**35th and 36th rows** As 1st and 2nd rows.
**37th and 38th rows** P17(19:19).
**39th and 40th rows** K17(19:19).
**41st to 44th rows** Work 1st to 4th rows.
**45th row** K7(8:8), K2 tog, yf, K8(9:9).
**46th row and 14 foll alt rows** P 17(19:19).
**47th row** K6(7:7), K2 tog, yf, K1, yf, sl 1, K1,
psso, K6(7:7).
**49th row** K5(6:6), K2 tog, yf, K3, yf, sl 1, K1,
psso, K5(6:6).
**51st row** K4(5:5), K2 tog, yf, K5, yf, sl 1, K1,
psso, K4(5:5).
**53rd row** K3(4:4), K2 tog, yf, K1, Tw2L, K1,
Tw2R, K1, yf, sl 1, K1, psso, K3(4:4).
**55th row** K2(3:3), K2 tog, yf, K1, Tw2L, K3,
Tw2R, K1, yf, sl 1, K1, psso, K2(3:3).
**57th row** K1(2:2), K2 tog, yf, K1, [Tw2L]
twice, K1, [Tw2R] twice, K1, yf, sl 1, K1, psso,
K1(2:2).

**59th row** K0(1:1), K2 tog, yf, K1, [Tw2L] twice, K3, [Tw2R] twice, K1, yf, sl 1, K1, psso, K0(1:1).

**61st row** K2(3:3), yf, sl 1, K1, psso, [Tw2L] twice, K1, [Tw2R] twice, K2 tog, yf, K2(3:3).

**63rd row** K3(4:4), yf, sl 1, K1, psso, Tw2L, K3, Tw2R, K2 tog, yf, K3(4:4).

**65th row** K4(5:5), yf, sl 1, K1, psso, Tw2L, K1, Tw2R, K2 tog, yf, K4(5:5).

**67th row** K5(6:6), yf, sl 1, K1, psso, K3, K2 tog, yf, K5(6:6).

**69th row** K6(7:7), yf, sl 1, K1, psso, K1, K2 tog, yf, K6(7:7).

**71st row** K7(8:8), yf, sl 1, K2 tog, psso, yf, K7(8:8).

**73rd row** K8(9:9), yf, sl 1, K1, psso, K7(8:8).

**75th to 82nd rows** Work 35th to 42nd rows.

**83rd row** As 5th row.

**84th row** P7(8:8), K1, P1, K1, P7(8:8).

**85th row** As 9th row.

**86th row** P5(6:6), K1, [P1, K1] 3 times, P5(6:6).

**87th row** As 13th row.

**88th row** P3(4:4), K1, P1, K1, P5, K1, P1, K1, P3(4:4).

**89th row** As 17th row.

**90th row** As 88th row.

**91st row** As 13th row.

**92nd row** As 86th row.

**93rd row** As 9th row.

**94th row** As 84th row.

**95th row** As 5th row.

**96th row** P17(19:19).

### PANEL B
WORKED OVER 13(13:15) STS

**1st row (right side)** K13(13:15).

**2nd row** P13(13:15).

**3rd row** K6(6:7), P1, K6(6:7).

**4th row and 5 foll alt rows** K the K sts, P the P sts as they appear.

**5th row** K5(5:6), P1, K1, P1, K5(5:6).

**7th row** K4(4:5), P1, [K1, P1] twice, K4(4:5).

**9th row** K3(3:4), P1, [K1, P1] 3 times, K3(3:4).

**11th row** K2(2:3), P1, K1, P1, K3, P1, K1, P1, K2(2:3).

**13th row** K1(1:2), P1, K1, P1, K5, P1, K1, P1, K1(1:2).

**15th row** K13(13:15).

**16th to 18th rows** P13(13:15).

**19th and 20th rows** K13(13:15).

**21st and 22nd rows** As 1st and 2nd rows.

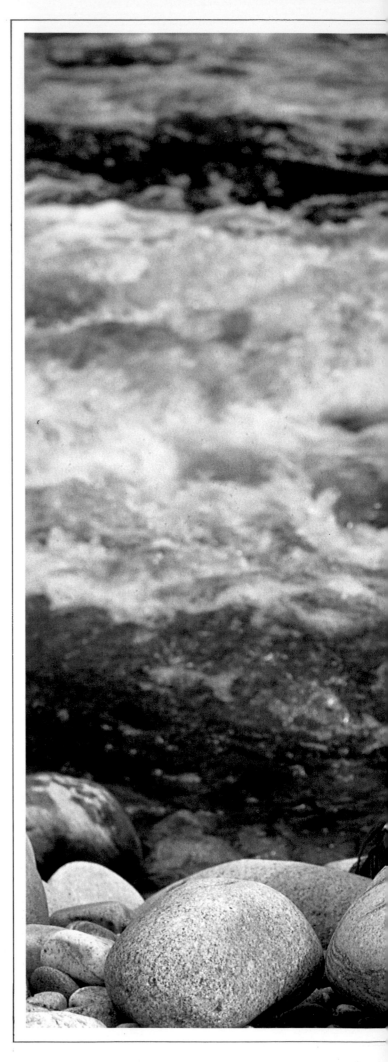

**23rd row** K2(2:3), [yf, sl 1, K1, psso] twice, K1, [K2 tog, yf] twice, K2(2:3).
**24th row and 5 foll alt rows** P13(13:15).
**25th row** K3(3:4), yf, sl 1, K1, psso, yf, sl 1, K2 tog, psso, yf, K2 tog, yf, K3(3:4).
**27th row** K4(4:5), yf, sl 1, K1, psso, yf, sl 1, K2 tog, psso, yf, K4(4:5).
**29th row** K5(5:6), [yf, sl 1, K1, psso] twice, K4(4:5).
**31st row** K3(3:4), K2 tog, yf, K1, [yf, sl 1, K1, psso] twice, K3(3:4).
**33rd row** K2(2:3), [K2 tog, yf] twice, K1, [yf, sl 1, K1, psso] twice, K2(2:3).
**35th row** K1(1:2), [K2 tog, yf] twice, K3, [yf, sl 1, K1, psso] twice, K1(1:2).
**36th to 42nd rows** Work 16th to 22nd rows.
**43rd row** As 3rd row.
**44th row** P5(5:6), K1, P1, K1, P5(5:6).
**45th row** As 7th row.
**46th row** P3(3:4), K1, [P1, K1] 3 times, P3(3:4).
**47th row** As 11th row.
**48th row** P1(1:2), K1, P1, K1, P5, K1, P1, K1, P1(1:2).
**49th row** As 3rd row.
**50th row** P5(5:6), K3, P5(5:6).
**51st row** K4(4:5), P5, K4(4:5).
**52nd row** P3(3:4), K7, P3(3:4).
**53rd row** K2(2:3), P9, K2(2:3).
**54th row** P1(1:2), K11, P1(1:2).
**55th row** K13(13:15).
**56th to 62nd rows** Work 16th to 22nd rows.
**63rd row** As 9th row.
**64th row** P4(4:5), K1, [P1, K1] twice, P4(4:5).
**65th row** As 5th row.
**66th row** P1(1:2), K1, [P4, K1] twice, P1(1:2).
**67th row** K2(2:3), P1, K7, P1, K2(2:3).
**68th row** P1(1:2), K1, P1, K1, P5, K1, P1, K1, P1(1:2).
**69th row** K2(2:3), P1, K1, P1, K3, P1, K1, P1, K2(2:3).
**70th row** As 68th row.
**71st row** As 67th row.
**72nd row** As 66th row.
**73rd row** As 5th row.
**74th row** as 64th row.
**75th row** As 9th row.
**76th to 82nd rows** Work 16th to 22nd rows.
**83rd row** K5(5:6), K2 tog, yf, K6(6:7).
**84th row and 5 foll alt rows** P13(13:15).
**85th row** K4(4:5), K2 tog, yf, K1, yf, sl 1, K1, psso, K4(4:5).

**87th row** K3(3:4), K2 tog, yf, K3, yf, sl 1, K1, psso, K3(3:4).
**89th row** As 33rd row.
**91st row** As 35th row.
**93rd row** K2(2:3), K2 tog, yf, K5, yf, sl 1, K1, psso, K2(2:3).
**95th row** K1(1:2), K2 tog, yf, K7, yf, sl 1, K1, psso, K1(1:2).
**96th row** P13(13:15).

## PANEL C
WORKED OVER 17 STS

**1st row (right side)** K17.
**2nd row** P17.
**3rd and 4th rows** As 1st and 2nd rows.
**5th row** K7, P1, K1, P1, K7.
**6th row** P6, K2, P1, K2, P6.
**7th row** K5, P2, K3, P2, K5.
**8th row** P4, K2, P5, K2, P4.
**9th row** K3, P2, K2, P1, K1, P1, K2, P2, K3.
**10th row** [P2, K2] twice, P1, [K2, P2] twice.
**11th row** K1, P2, K2, P2, K3, P2, K2, P2, K1.
**12th row** P1, K1, P2, K2, P5, K2, P2, K1, P1.
**13th and 14th rows** As 9th and 10th rows.
**15th row** K2, P1, K2, P2, K3, P2, K2, P1, K2.
**16th and 17th rows** As 8th and 9th rows.
**18th row** P3, K1, P2, K2, P1, K2, P2, K1, P3.
**19th and 20th rows** As 7th and 8th rows.
**21st row** K4, P1, K2, P1, K1, P1, K2, P1, K4.
**22nd and 23rd rows** As 6th and 7th rows.
**24th row** P5, [K1, P5] twice.
**25th and 26th rows** As 5th and 6th rows.
**27th row** K6, P1, K3, P1, K6.
**28th row** P8, K1, P8.
**29th row** K8, P1, K8.
**30th row** P7, K1, P1, K1, P7.
**31st row** As 5th row.
**32nd and 33rd rows** As 28th and 29th rows.
**34th row** P17.
**35th and 36th rows** As 1st and 2nd rows.
**37th and 38th rows** P17.
**39th and 40th rows** K17.
**41st to 44th rows** Work 1st to 4th rows.
**45th row** K7, K2 tog, yf, K8.
**46th row and 13 foll alt rows** P17.
**47th row** K6, K2 tog, yf, K1, yf, sl 1, K1, psso, K6.
**49th row** K5, K2 tog, yf, K3, yf, sl 1, K1, psso, K5.
**51st row** K4, K2 tog, yf, K5, yf, sl 1, K1, psso, K4.

**53rd row** K3, [K2 tog, yf, K1] twice, [yf, sl 1, K1, psso, K1] twice, K2.

**55th row** K2, [K2 tog, yf, K1] twice, K2, [yf, sl 1, K1, psso, K1] twice, K1.

**57th row** As 51st row.

**59th row** As 53rd row.

**61st row** As 49th row.

**63rd row** As 51st row.

**65th row** As 47th row.

**67th row** As 49th row.

**69th row** As 45th row.

**71st row** As 47th row.

**73rd row** As 45th row.

**74th to 82nd rows** Work 34th to 42nd rows.

**83rd row** As 29th row.

**84th row** P7, K3, P7.

**85th row** K6, P2, K1, P2, K6.

**86th row** P5, K2, P3, K2, P5.

**87th row** K4, P2, K5, P2, K4.

**88th row** P3, K2, P7, K2, P3.

**89th row** K2, P2, K9, P2, K2.

**90th row** As 88th row.

**91st row** As 87th row.

**92nd row** As 86th row.

**93rd row** As 85th row.

**94th row** As 84th row.

**95th row** As 29th row.

**96th row** P17.

## MAIN PART
### KNITTED IN ONE PIECE TO ARMHOLES

With 2¾mm (No 12/US 2) circular needle, cast on 272(296:320) sts. Mark end of cast on row to denote end of rounds. Taking care not to twist the work, cont as follows:

**1st round** [P1, K2, P1] to end.

Rep this round until work measures 8cm/3in from beg.

**Next round** * Rib 8(4:8), [work twice in next st, rib 9(9:8) sts] 12(14:16) times, work twice in next st, rib 7(3:7) rep from * once more. 298(326:354) sts.

Change to 3mm (No 11/US 3) circular needle. K1 round. P 2 rounds. K 1 round.

Work in bodice patt as follows:

**1st and 2nd rounds** * P1, [K15(17:19), P2, K3, P2] 6 times, K15(17:19), P1; rep from * once more.

**3rd and 4th rounds** * P1, [K7(8:9), P1, K7(8:9), P7] 6 times, K7(8:9), P1, K7(8:9), P1; rep from * once more.

**5th and 6th rounds** * P1, [K6(7:8), P1, K1, P1, K6(7:8), P2, K3, P2] 6 times, K6(7:8), P1, K1, P1, K6(7:8), P1; rep from * once more.

**7th and 8th rounds** * P1, [K5(6:7), P1, K1, P1, K1, P1, K5(6:7), P7] 6 times, K5(6:7), P1, [K1, P1] twice, K5(6:7), P1; rep from * once more.

**9th and 10th rounds** * P1, [K4(5:6), P1, K1, P1, K1, P1, K1, P1, K4(5:6), P2, K3, P2] 6 times, K4(5:6), P1, [K1, P1] 3 times, K4(5:6), P1; rep from * once more.

**11th and 12th rounds** * P1, [K3(4:5), P1, K1, P1, K3, P1, K1, P1, K3(4:5), P7] 6 times, K3(4:5), P1, K1, P1, K3, P1, K1, P1, K3(4:5), P1; rep from * once more.

**13th and 14th rounds** * P1, [K2(3:4), P1, K1, P1, K5, P1, K1, P1, K2(3:4), P2, K3, P2] 6 times, K2(3:4), P1, K1, P1, K5, P1, K1, P1, K2(3:4), P1; rep from * once more.

**15th and 16th rounds** * P1, [K1(2:3), P1, K1, P1, K7, P1, K1, P1, K1(2:3), P7] 6 times, K1(2:3), P1, K1, P1, K7, P1, K1, P1, K1(2:3), P1; rep from * once more.

These 16 rounds form bodice patt. Rep these 16 rounds 6 times more then work 1st and 2nd rounds again. K 1 round. P 2 rounds. K 1 round. Work border patt as follows:

**1st and 2nd rounds** * P1, K147(161:175), P1; rep from * once more.

**3rd round** * P1, K2(1:4), [P2, K6] 18(20:21) times, K1(0:3), P1; rep from * once more.

**4th round** * P1, K2(1:4), [K1, P2, K5] 18(20:21) times, K1(0:3), P1; rep from * once more.

**5th round** * P1, K2(1:4), [K2, P2, K4] 18(20:21) times, K1(0:3), P1; rep from * once more.

**6th round** * P1, K2(1:4), [K3, P2, K3] 18(20:21) times, K1(0:3), P1; rep from * once more.

**7th round** * P1, K2(1:4), [K4, P2, K2] 18(20:21) times, K1(0:3), P1; rep from * once more.

**8th round** * P1, K2(1:4), [K5, P2, K1] 18(20:21) times, K1(0:3), P1; rep from * once more.

**9th round** As 7th round.
**10th round** As 6th round.
**11th round** As 5th round.
**12th round** As 4th round.
**13th round** As 3rd round.
**14th and 15th rounds** As 1st and 2nd rounds.

### Divide work as follows

**Next row** K149(163:177), turn. Work backwards and forwards on this set of sts only for Back. K 1 row. P 1 row.

**Next row** P29(36:40), [m1, P2] twice, P24(24:27), [m1, P2] twice, P27, [P2, m1] twice, P24(24:27), [P2, m1] twice, P29(36:40). 157(171:185) sts.

Work in yoke patt as follows:

**1st row (right side)** P2, K2(7:10), P2, work 1st row of Panel A, * P2, K2 tog, yrn, P1, K6(6:8), P1, yon, sl 1, K1, psso, P2 *; work 1st row of Panel B, ** P2, K2 tog, yrn, P1, K8, P1, yon, sl 1, K1, psso, P2 **; work 1st

row of Panel C, rep from ** to ** once, work 1st row of Panel B, rep from * to * once, work 1st row of Panel A, P2, K2(7:10), P2.

**2nd row** K2, P2(7:10), K2, work 2nd row of Panel A, * K2, P2, K1, P6(6:8), K1, P2, K2*; work 2nd row of Panel B, ** K2, P2, K1, P8, K1, P2, K2 **; work 2nd row of Panel C, rep from ** to ** once, work 2nd row of Panel B, rep from * to * once, work 2nd row of Panel A, K2, P2(7:10), K2.

**3rd row** P6(11:14), work 3rd row of Panel A, * P2, yon, sl 1, K1, psso, P1, C6(C6:C8), P1, K2 tog, yrn, P2 *; work 3rd row of Panel B, ** P2, yon, sl 1, K1, psso, P1, C8, P1, K2 tog, yrn, P2 **; work 3rd row of Panel C, rep from ** to ** once, work 3rd row of Panel B, rep from * to * once, work 3rd row of Panel A, P6(11:14).

**4th row** K6(11:14), work 4th row of Panel A, * K2, P2, K1, P6(6:8), K1, P2, K2 *; work 4th row of Panel B, ** K2, P2, K1, P8, K1, P2, K2 **; work 4th row of Panel C, rep from ** to ** once, work 4th row of Panel B, rep from * to * once, work 4th row of Panel A, K6(11:14).

These 4 rows set yoke patt. Cont in yoke patt, working appropriate rows of Panels until 96th row of Panels has been worked. P 2 rows. Leave these sts on a spare needle.

With right side facing, rejoin yarn to rem sts for Front, K to end. Work as given for Back until 76th row of Panels has been worked.

### Shape Neck

**Next row** Patt 62(68:74), turn. Work on this set of sts only.

Keeping patt correct, dec one st at neck edge on next 8 rows. 54(60:66) sts.

Patt 11 rows straight. P 2 rows.

Work shoulder gusset as follows:

**1st row (right side)** K1(3:1), [P2, K2] to last st, K1.

**2nd row** P1, [P2, K2] to last 1(3:1) sts, P1(3:1).

**3rd row** P1(3:1), [K2, P2] to last st, P1.

**4th row** K1, [K2, P2] to last 1(3:1) sts, K1(3:1).

Rep last 4 rows 1(3:7) times more. Leave these sts on a spare needle.

With right side facing, sl centre 33(35:37) sts onto a holder, rejoin yarn to rem sts and patt to end. Complete to match first side.

### Join Shoulders

With wrong sides of Back and Front together and Front facing, cast off together knitwise 54(60:66) shoulder sts (see diagram page 39), leaving centre 49(51:53) back neck sts on a holder.

### SLEEVES

With set of four 3mm (No 11/US 3) needles and right side facing, pick up and K149(163:177) sts evenly around armhole edge. Mark end of last round to denote end of rounds. P 2 rounds. K 1 round.

Work in rounds and patt as follows:

**1st and 2nd rounds** As 1st and 2nd rounds of bodice patt as given for Main Part but working from * once.

These 2 rounds set patt. Beg with 16th round and working rounds in reverse order (from 16th to 1st round), work in patt as set, **at the same time**, dec one st inside the border of one (P) st at each end of 10th(1st:1st) and every foll 3rd round until 69(77:91) sts rem. Patt 1 round. K 1 round. P 2 rounds.

Change to set of four 2¾mm (No 12/US 2) needles.

**Next round** K1(3:0), [K2 tog, K2(2:1), K 2 tog, K2(1:1) sts] to last 4(4:7) sts, K2 tog, K2, [K3 tog] 0(0:1) time. 52(56:60) sts.

**Next round** [P1, K2, P1] to end.

Rep this round for 7cm/2¾in. Cast off in rib.

### NECKBAND

With 2¾mm (No 12/US 2) circular needle and beg at centre of left front gusset, pick up and K24(26:32) sts down left front neck, K across 33(35:37) centre front neck sts, pick up and K24(26:32) sts up right front neck to centre of gusset, 4(6:8) sts down right back neck, K across 49(51:53) centre back neck sts, pick up and K4(6:8) sts up left back neck, then 4 sts behind first 4 picked up sts. 142(154:174) sts.

Work backwards and forwards as follows:

**1st row (wrong side)** K.

**2nd and 3rd rows** P.

**4th row** K6, [P2, K2] to last 4 sts, K4.

**5th row** K4, [P2, K2] to last 2 sts, K2.

**6th row (buttonhole)** K1, K2 tog, yf, K3, [P2, K2] to last 4 sts, K4.

**7th row** As 5th row.

**8th to 11th rows** Rep 4th and 5th rows twice.

Rep 4th to 11th rows once more, then work 4th to 9th rows again. Cast off in patt.

### TO COMPLETE

Sew on buttons.

## MATERIALS

10(11) 100g balls of Wilkinsons
Guernsey 5 ply.
1 pair in each of 2¼mm (No 13/US 2)
and 3mm (No 11/US 4) knitting
needles.
Cable needle.

## MEASUREMENTS

To fit bust 81-91(97-107)cm
32-36(38-42)in
All round at bust 112(125)cm
44(49¼)in
Length to shoulder 69(72)cm
27(28¼)in
Sleeve seam 44(46)cm/17¼(18)in

## TENSION

26 sts and 38 rows to 10cm/4in square
measured over st st on 3mm (No 11/
US 4) needles.

## ABBREVIATIONS

See page 8.

# LACE AND CABLE GANSEY

-+-

### PANEL A
WORKED OVER 13 STS

**1st row (right side)** K13.
**2nd row** P10, K2, P1.
**3rd row** K2, P2, K9.
**4th row** P8, K2, P3.
**5th row** K4, P2, K7.
**6th row** P6, K2, P5.
**7th row** K6, P2, K5.
**8th row** P4, K2, P7.
**9th row** K8, P2, K3.
**10th row** P2, K2, P9.
**11th row** K10, P2, K1.
**12th row** P13.
These 12 rows form patt.

### PANEL B
WORKED OVER 13 STS

**1st row (right side)** K6, P1, K6.
**2nd row** P5, K3, P5.
**3rd row** K4, P5, K4.
**4th row** P3, K7, P3.
**5th row** K2, P9, K2.
**6th row** P1, K11, P1.
**7th row** As 5th row.
**8th row** As 4th row.
**9th row** As 3rd row.
**10th row** As 2nd row.
**11th row** As 1st row.
**12th row** P13.
**13th row** As 1st row.
**14th row** P5, K1, P1, K1, P5.
**15th row** K4, P1, [K1, P1] twice, K4.
**16th row** P3, K1, [P1, K1] 3 times, P3.
**17th row** K2, P1, [K1, P1] 4 times, K2.
**18th row** P1, [K1, P1] 6 times.
**19th row** As 17th row.
**20th row** As 16th row.
**21st row** As 15th row.
**22nd row** As 14th row.
**23rd row** As 1st row.
**24th row** P13.
These 24 rows form patt.

## PANEL C

WORKED OVER 8 STS

**1st row (right side)** P2, K4, P2.
**2nd row** K2, P4, K2.
**3rd row** P2, sl next 2 sts onto cable needle and leave at back, K2, then K2 from cable needle, P2.
**4th row** As 2nd row.
These 4 rows form patt.

## PANEL D

WORKED OVER 11 STS

**1st row (right side)** K1, yf, sl 1, K1, psso, K5, K2 tog, yf, K1.
**2nd and every foll alt row** P11.
**3rd row** K2, yf, sl 1, K1, psso, K3, K2 tog, yf, K2.
**5th row** K3, yf, sl 1, K1, psso, K1, K2 tog, yf, K3.
**7th row** K4, yf, sl 1, K2 tog, psso, yf, K4.
**9th row** K3, K2 tog, yf, K1, yf, sl 1, K1, psso, K3.
**11th row** K2, K2 tog, yf, K3, yf, sl 1, K1, psso, K2.
**13th row** K1, K2 tog, yf, K5, yf, sl 1, K1, psso, K1.
**15th row** K2 tog, yf, K7, yf, sl 1, K1, psso.
**16th row** P11.
These 16 rows form patt.

## PANEL E

WORKED OVER 9 STS

**1st row (right side)** K1, yf, K2, sl 1, K2 tog, psso, K2, yf, K1.
**2nd and foll alt row** P9.
**3rd row** K2, yf, K1, sl 1, K2 tog, psso, K1, yf, K2.
**5th row** K3, yf, sl 1, K2 tog, psso, yf, K3.
**6th row** P9.
These 6 rows form patt.

## BACK

With 2¼mm (No 13/US 2) needles cast on 134(150) sts.
**1st row (right side)** K2, [P2, K2] to end.
**2nd row** P2, [K2, P2] to end.
Rep these 2 rows until work measures 8cm/3in from beg, ending with a right side row.
**Next row** Rib 3(2), [inc in next st, rib 6(7) sts] to last 5(4) sts, inc in next st, rib 4(3). 153(169) sts.

Change to 3mm (No 11/US 4) needles. Work in bodice patt as follows:
**1st row (right side)** K10(3), work 1st row of Panel A, [K2, work 1st row of Panel B, K2, work 1st row of Panel A] 4(5) times, K10(3).
**2nd row** K10(3), work 2nd row of Panel A, [K2, work 2nd row of Panel B, K2, work 2nd row of Panel A] 4(5) times, K10(3).
**3rd row** K10(3), work 3rd of Panel A, [K2, work 3rd row of Panel B, K2, work 3rd row of Panel A] 4(5) times, K10(3).
**4th row** P8(1), K2, work 4th row of Panel A, [K2, work 4th row of Panel B, K2, work 4th row of Panel A] 4(5) times, K2, P8(1).
These 4 rows set bodice patt. Cont in bodice patt, working appropriate rows of Panels until work measures 39(42)cm/15¼(16½)in from beg, ending with a 24th (12th) row of Panels. Work border patt as follows: K 5 rows.
**1st row (wrong side)** P4(3), K1, [P5, K1] to last 4(3) sts, P4(3).
**2nd row** K3(2), P1, K1, P1, [K3, P1, K1, P1] to last 3(2) sts, K3(2).
**3rd row** P2(1), [K1, P3, K1, P1] to last 1(0) st, P1(0).
**4th row** K1(0), P1, [K5, P1] to last 1(0) st, K1(0).
**5th row** As 3rd row.
**6th row** As 2nd row.
**7th row** As 1st row. K 3 rows.
**Next row** K8(4), [K twice in next st, K7(6) sts] to last 9(4) sts, K twice in next st, K8(3). 171(193) sts.
Now work in yoke patt as follows:
**1st row (right side)** [P2, work 1st row of Panel E] 0(1) time, [work 1st row of Panel C, Panel D, Panel C and Panel E] 4 times, work 1st row of Panel C, Panel D and Panel C, [work 1st row of Panel E, P2] 0(1) time.
**2nd row** [K2, work 2nd row of Panel E] 0(1) time, [work 2nd row of Panel C, Panel D, Panel C and Panel E] 4 times, work 2nd row of Panel C, Panel D and Panel C, [work 2nd row of Panel E, K2] 0(1) time.
These 2 rows set yoke patt. Cont in yoke patt, working appropriate rows of Panels until work measures 69(72)cm/27(28¼)in from beg, ending with a wrong side row.

### *Shape Shoulders*

Cast off 29(33) sts at beg of next 4 rows. Leave rem 55(61) sts on a holder.

Cont without shaping until work measures same as Back to shoulder shaping, ending at side edge.

### Shape Shoulder

Cast off 29(33) sts at beg of next row. Work 1 row. Cast off rem 29(33) sts.

With right side facing, sl centre 29(33) sts onto a holder, rejoin yarn to rem sts and patt to end. Complete to match first side.

### SLEEVES

With 2¼mm (No 13/US 2) needles cast on 58(66) sts.

Work in rib as given for Back for 8cm/3in, ending with a right side row.

**Next row** Rib 0(3), [inc in next st, rib 1(2) sts] to end. 87 sts.

Change to 3mm (No 11/US 4) needles. Work in patt as follows:

**1st row** P2, work 1st row of Panel D, [work 1st row of Panel C, Panel E, Panel C and Panel D] twice, P2.

**2nd row** K2, work 2nd row of Panel D, [work 2nd row of Panel C, Panel E, Panel C and Panel D] twice, K2.

These 2 rows set patt. Cont in patt, working appropriate rows of Panels, **at the same time**, inc one st at each end of next and every foll 4th row until there are 143(147) sts, working inc sts into patt.

Cont without shaping until work measures 44(46)cm/17¼(18)in from beg, ending with a wrong side row. Cast off.

### NECKBAND

Join right shoulder seam.

With 2¼mm (No 13/US 2) needles and right side facing, pick up and K 27 sts down left front neck, K across 29(33) centre front sts dec 2(3) sts evenly, pick up and K 27 sts up right front neck, K across 55(61) sts at back neck dec 6(7) sts evenly. 130(138) sts.

Beg with a 2nd row, work 13 rows in rib as given for Back. Cast off in rib.

### TO MAKE UP

Join left shoulder and neckband seam. Sew on sleeves, placing centre of sleeves to shoulder seams. Join side and sleeve seams.

### FRONT

Work as given for Back until work measures 60(63)cm/23½(24¾)in from beg, ending with a wrong side row.

### Shape Neck

**Next row** Patt 71(80), turn. Work on this set of sts only.

Keeping patt correct, dec one st at neck edge on next 4 rows, then on every alt row until 58(66) sts rem.

## MATERIALS

10(11:11) 100g balls of Hayfield Brig
Aran.
1 pair in each of 4mm (No 8/US 6) and
5mm (No 6/US 8) knitting needles.
One 4mm (No 8/US 6) circular needle,
100cm long.
Cable needle.
9 buttons.

## MEASUREMENTS

To fit bust 86(91:97)cm/34(36:38)in
All round at bust 118(122:127)cm
46½(48:50)in
Length to shoulder 69(70:71)cm
27(27½:28)in
Sleeve seam 44(45:46)cm
17¼(17¾:18)in

## TENSION

18 sts and 24 rows to 10cm/4in square
measured over st st on 5mm (No 6/
US 8) needles.

## ABBREVIATIONS

Cr2R-sl next st onto cable needle and
leave at back, K1, then P1 from cable
needle.
Cr2L-sl next st onto cable needle and
leave at front, P1, then K1 from cable
needle.
C3-sl next 2 sts onto cable needle and
leave at back, K1, sl first st on cable
needle back onto left-hand needle and
P this st, then K1 from cable needle.
Also see page 8.

# ARAN
JACKET
WITH LACE
PANELS

### PANEL A

REP OF 2 STS PLUS 1 ST

**1st and 2nd rows** K.
**3rd row (right side)** K1, ★ yf, K2 tog; rep
from ★.
**4th and 5th rows** K.
**6th row** P.
These 6 rows form patt.

### PANEL B

WORKED OVER 12 STS

**1st row (right side)** P2, sl next 2 sts onto cable
needle and leave at back, K2, then K2 from
cable needle, sl next 2 sts onto cable needle and
leave at front, K2, then K2 from cable needle,
P2.
**2nd and foll alt row** K2, P8, K2.
**3rd row** P2, K8, P2.
**5th row** As 3rd row.
**6th row** As 2nd row.
These 6 rows form patt.

### PANEL C

WORKED OVER 19 STS

**1st row (right side)** K1, yf, K2 tog, P2, K1,
yf, K2, sl 1, K2 tog, psso, K2, yf, K1, P2, yb,
sl 1, K1, psso, yf, K1.
**2nd and foll alt row** P3, K2, P9, K2, P3.
**3rd row** K1, yf, K2 tog, P2, K2, yf, K1, sl 1,
K2 tog, psso, K1, yf, K2, P2, yb, sl 1, K1, psso,
yf, K1.
**5th row** K1, yf, K2 tog, P2, K3, yf, sl 1, K2
tog, psso, yf, K3, P2, yb, sl 1, K1, psso, yf, K1.
**6th row** As 2nd row.
These 6 rows form patt.

### PANEL D

REP OF 8 STS

**1st row (right side)** ★ P2, Cr2R, Cr2L, P2;
rep from ★.
**2nd row** ★ K2, [P1, K2] twice; rep from ★.
**3rd row** ★ P1, Cr2R, P2, Cr2L, P1; rep from ★.
**4th row** ★ K1, P1, K4, P1, K1; rep from ★.
**5th row** ★ Cr2R, P4, Cr2L; rep from ★.

**6th row** * P1, K6, P1; rep from *.
**7th row** * Cr2L, P4, Cr2R; rep from *.
**8th row** As 4th row.
**9th row** P1, Cr2L, P2, Cr2R, P1; rep from *.
**10th row** As 2nd row.
**11th row** * P2, Cr2L, Cr2R, P2; rep from *.
**12th row** * K3, P2, K3; rep from *.
These 12 rows form patt.

### BACK

With 4mm (No 8/US 6) needles cast on 103(109:113) sts.
**\*\*Work in welt patt as follows:**
**1st row (right side)** [P1, K1] 3(2:3) times, yf, K2 tog, * [P1, K1] 4 times, yf, K2 tog; rep from * to last 5(3:5) sts, P1, [K1, P1] 2(1:2) times.
**2nd row** K1, [P1, K1] to end.
**3rd and 4th rows** As 1st and 2nd rows.
**5th row** P1, [K1, P1] 2 (1:2) times, C3, * P1, [K1, P1] 3 times, C3; rep from * to last 5(3:5) sts, P1, [K1, P1] 2(1:2) times.
**6th row** As 2nd row.
**7th and 8th rows** As 1st and 2nd rows.
Rep these 8 rows once more, then work 1st to 6th rows again.
Change to 5mm (No 6/US 8) needles.
Beg with a 1st row, work 9 rows of Panel A across all sts for border patt. **\*\***
**Next row** K9(14:16), K twice in next st, [K6(7:7), K twice in next st] to last 9(14:16) sts, K to end. 116(120:124) sts.
Work in main patt as follows:
**1st row (right side)** Work 5th row of Panel A across first 9(11:13) sts, work 1st row of Panel B, then Panel C, P2, work 1st row of Panel D across next 32 sts, P2, work 1st row of Panel C, then Panel B, work 5th row of Panel A across last 9(11:13) sts.
**2nd row** Work 6th row of Panel A across first 9(11:13) sts, work 2nd row of Panel B, then Panel C, K2, work 2nd row of Panel D across next 32 sts, K2, work 2nd row of Panel C, then Panel B, work 6th row of Panel A across last 9(11:13) sts.
These 2 rows set main patt. Cont in main patt, working appropriate rows of Panels until work measures 69(70:71)cm/27(27½:28)in from beg, ending with a wrong side row. Cast off.

### LEFT FRONT

With 4mm (No 8/US 6) needles cast on 53(55:57) sts.

Work in welt patt as follows:
**1st row (right side)** * [P1, K1] 3(2:3) times, yf, K2 tog, [P1, K1] 1(2:1) times; rep from * to last 3(5:7) sts, [P1, K1] 1(2:3) times, P1.
**2nd row** K1, [P1, K1] to end.
**3rd and 4th rows** As 1st and 2nd rows.
**5th row** * P1, [K1, P1] 2(1:2) times, C3, [P1, K1] 1(2:1) times; rep from * to last 3(5:7) sts, [P1, K1] 1(2:3) times, P1.
**\*\*\* 6th row** As 2nd row.
**7th and 8th rows** As 1st and 2nd rows.
Rep these 8 rows once more, then work 1st to 6th rows again.
Change to 5mm (No 6/US 8) needles.
Beg with a 1st row, work 9 rows of Panel A across all sts for border patt. **\*\*\***
**Next row** K2, [K twice in next st, K6] 6 times, K9(11:13). 59(61:63) sts.
Work in main patt as follows:
**1st row (right side)** Work 5th row of Panel A across first 9(11:13) sts, work 1st row of Panel B, then Panel C, P2, work 1st row of Panel D across next 16 sts, P1.
**2nd row** K1, work 2nd row of Panel D across next 16 sts, K2, work 2nd row of Panel C, then Panel B, work 6th row of Panel A across last 9(11:13) sts.
These 2 rows set main patt. Cont in main patt, working appropriate rows of Panels until work measures 44(45:46)cm/17¼(17¾:18)in from beg, ending with a wrong side row.

### *Shape Front*

Keeping patt correct, dec one st at end (front edge) of next row and at same edge on every foll 3rd row until 41(43:45) sts rem.
Cont without shaping until work measures same as Back to cast off edge, ending with a wrong side row. Cast off.

### RIGHT FRONT

With 4mm (No 8/US 6) needles cast on 53(55:57) sts. Work in welt patt as follows:
**1st row (right side)** P1, [K1, P1] 1(2:3) times, * [K1, P1] 1(2:1) times, K1, yf, K2 tog, P1, [K1, P1] 2(1:2) times; rep from * to end.
**2nd row** K1, [P1, K1] to end.
**3rd and 4th rows** As 1st and 2nd rows.
**5th row** P1, [K1, P1] 1(2:3) times, * [K1, P1] 1(2:1) times, C3, P1, [K1, P1] 2(1:2) times; rep from * to end.
Now work as given for Left Front from **\*\*\*** to **\*\*\***.

**Next row** K9(11:13), [K6, K twice in next st] 6 times, K2. 59(61:63) sts.

Work in main patt as follows:

**1st row (right side)** P1, work 1st row of Panel D across next 16 sts, P2, work 1st row of Panel C, then Panel B, work 5th row of Panel A across last 9(11:13) sts.

**2nd row** Work 6th row of Panel A across first 9(11:13) sts, work 2nd row of Panel B, then Panel C, K2, work 2nd row of Panel D across next 16 sts, K1.

Complete as Left Front, reversing front shaping.

### SLEEVES

With 4mm (No 8/US 6) needles cast on 49 sts. Work as given for 2nd size on Back from ★★ to ★★.

**Next row** K4, [K twice in next st, K9] 4 times, K twice in next st, K4. 54 sts.

Work in main patt as follows:

**1st row (right side)** K1, ★ P2, K1, yf, K2, sl 1, K2 tog, psso, K2, yf, K1, P2 ★; yb, sl 1, K1, psso, yf, K1 (part of 1st row of Panel C), P2, work 1st row of Panel D across next 16 sts, P2, K1, yf, K2 tog, rep from ★ to ★ once, K1.

**2nd row** P1, K2, P9, K2, P3, K2, work 2nd row of Panel D across next 16 sts, K2, P3, K2, P9, K2, P1.

These 2 rows set main patt. Cont in main patt, working appropriate rows of Panels, **at the same time**, inc one st at each end of next and every foll alt row until there are 58(66:74) sts, then on every foll 3rd row until there are 96(100:104) sts, working inc sts into patt to match Back.

Cont without shaping until work measures 44(45:46)cm/17¼(17¾:18)in from beg, ending with a wrong side row. Cast off.

### FRONT BAND

Join shoulder seams.

With 4mm (No 8/US 6) circular needle and right side facing, pick up and K86(88:91) sts up straight edge of Right Front, 52 sts up shaped edge, 33 sts across back neck, 52 sts down shaped edge of Left Front and 86(88:91) sts down straight edge. 309(313:319) sts. Work backwards and forwards.

Beg with a 4th row and following 2nd(1st:2nd) size, work 11 rows in welt patt as given for Back. Cast off in rib.

### TO MAKE UP

Sew on sleeves, placing centre of sleeves to shoulder seams. Join side and sleeve seams. Sew on buttons (use eyelet holes of welt pattern as buttonholes).

## MATERIALS

13(14) 100g balls of Hayfield Brig Aran.
1 pair in each of 3¾mm (No 9/US 6)
and 4½mm (No 7/US 8) knitting
needles.
Set of four 3¾mm (No 9/US 6) double
pointed knitting needles.
Cable needle.

## MEASUREMENTS

To fit bust or chest 81-97(102-117)cm
32-38(40-46)in
All round at bust or chest
116(142)cm/45½(56)in
Length to shoulder 68(72)cm
26¾(28¼)in
Sleeve seam 45(48)cm/17¾(19)in

## TENSION

19 sts and 25 rows to 10cm/4in square
measured over st st on 4½mm (No 7/
US 8) needles.

## ABBREVIATIONS

C4B-sl next 2 sts onto cable needle and
leave at back, K2, then K2 from cable
needle.
C4F-sl next 2 sts onto cable needle and
leave at front, K2, then K2 from cable
needle.
C6B-sl next 3 sts onto cable needle and
leave at back, K3, then K3 from cable
needle.
C6F-sl next 3 sts onto cable needle and
leave at front, K3, then K3 from cable
needle.
Also see page 8.

# FISHERMAN'S STYLE SWEATER

## PANEL A

WORKED OVER 17 STS

**1st row (right side)** P2, K13, P2.
**2nd row** K2, P6, K1, P6, K2.
**3rd row** P2, K5, P1, K1, P1, K5, P2.
**4th row** K2, P4, [K1, P1] twice, K1, P4, K2.
**5th row** P2, K3, [P1, K1] 3 times, P1, K3, P2.
**6th row** K2, P2, [K1, P1] 4 times, K1, P2, K2.
**7th row** P2, K1, [P1, K1] 6 times, P2.
**8th row** As 6th row.
**9th row** As 5th row.
**10th row** As 4th row.
**11th row** As 3rd row.
**12th row** As 2nd row.
These 12 rows form patt.

## PANEL B

WORKED OVER 24 STS

**1st row (right side)** K4, P2, K12, P2, K4.
**2nd row** P4, K2, P12, K2, P4.
**3rd row** C4B, P2, C6B, C6F, P2, C4F.
**4th row** As 2nd row.
**5th and 6th rows** As 1st and 2nd rows.
**7th row** C4B, P2, K12, P2, C4F.
**8th row** As 2nd row.
**9th and 10th rows** As 1st and 2nd rows.
**11th row** As 3rd row.
**12th row** As 2nd row.
These 12 rows form patt.

## BACK

With 3¾mm (No 9/US 6) needles cast on
98(118) sts.
**1st row (right side)** K2, [P2, K2] to end.
**2nd row** P2, [K2, P2] to end.
Rep these 2 rows until work measures 8cm/3in
from beg, ending with a right side row.
**Next row** Rib 1(3), m1, [rib 8(7), m1] 12(16)
times, rib to end. 111(135) sts.
Change to 4½mm (No 7/US 8) needles.
Beg with a K row, work in st st until work
measures 37cm/14½in from beg, ending with a
P row. K 5 rows.
**Next row** K7(12), [m1, K2, m1, K3] 20(23)
times, K to end. 151(181) sts.
Work in yoke patt as follows:

**1st row (right side)** P2(0), [work 1st row of Panel B(A), then Panel A(B)] 3(4) times, work 1st row of Panel B(A), P2(0).

**2nd row** K2(0), [work 2nd row of Panel B(A), then Panel A(B)] 3(4) times, work 2nd row of Panel B(A), K2(0).

These 2 rows set patt. Cont in patt as set, working appropriate rows of Panels until work measures 64(68)cm/25¼(26¾)in from beg, ending with 12th row of Panels.

### Shape Shoulders

Cast off 48(60) sts at beg of next 2 rows. Leave rem 55(61) sts on a holder.

### FRONT

Work as given for Back until work measures 60(64)cm/23¾(25¼)in from beg, ending with a wrong side row.

### Shape Neck

**Next row** Patt 63(76), turn. Work on this set of sts only.

Keeping patt correct, cast off 4 sts at beg of next and foll 2 alt rows. Dec one st at neck edge on next 3(4) rows. 48(60) sts.

Cont without shaping for a few rows until work measures same as Back to shoulder shaping, ending at side edge. Cast off.

With right side facing, slip centre 25(29) sts onto a holder, rejoin yarn to rem sts and patt to end. Patt 1 row. Complete to match first side.

### SLEEVES

With 3¾mm (No 9/US 6) needles cast on 42(46) sts. Work 8cm/3in in rib as given for Back, ending with a right side row.
**Next row** Rib 4(1), m1, [rib 3(4), m1] 11 times, rib 5(1). 54(58) sts.
Change to 4½mm (No 7/US 8) needles.

Beg with a K row, work in st st, inc one st at each end of 5th and every foll 4th row until there are 74(78) sts. Work 3 rows straight. K 5 rows.
**Next row** K11(13), m1, [K4, m1] 13 times, K11(13). 88(92) sts.
Work in patt as follows:
**1st row (right side)** K15(17), work 1st row of Panel A, Panel B and Panel A, K15(17).
**2nd row** P15(17), work 2nd row of Panel A, Panel B and Panel A, P15(17).
These 2 rows set patt. Cont in patt as set, working appropriate rows of Panels, **at the same time**, inc one st at each end of next and every foll 4th row until there are 110(118) sts, working inc sts into st st.
Cont without shaping until work measures 45(48)cm/17¾(19)in from beg, ending with a wrong side row.

#### Shape Saddle

Keeping patt correct, cast off 41(45) sts at beg of next 2 rows. 28 sts.
Cont in patt on rem sts for saddle shoulder until saddle, when slightly stretched, fits across cast off shoulder sts on Back or Front, ending with a wrong side row. Leave these sts on a holder.

### COLLAR

Sew row ends of saddles to Back and Front shoulders.
With set of four 3¾mm (No 9/US 6) needles and right side facing, [K2 tog] 14 times across left saddle sts, pick up and K14(15) sts down left front neck, K centre front sts dec 9 sts evenly, pick up and K 14(15) sts up right front neck, [K2 tog] 14 times across right saddle sts, K back neck sts dec 23 sts evenly. 104(116) sts.
Work 12cm/4¾in in rounds of K2, P2 rib. Cast off in rib.

### TO MAKE UP

Sew on sleeves. Join side and sleeve seams.

## MATERIALS

7(7:8) 1oz hanks of Jamiesons Pure
Shetland in Granite (122) M.
2×1oz hanks of same in each of Fjord
(170) A, Rey (140) C, Mogit (107) D and
Twilight (175) E.
1×2oz hank of Natural White (104) B.
One in each of 2¼mm (No 13/US 1)
and 3mm (No 11/US 3) circular
needles, 80cm long.
One set of four in each of 2¼mm
(No 13/US 1) and 3mm (No 11/US 3)
double pointed knitting needles.

## MEASUREMENTS

To fit bust 86-91(97-102:107-112)cm
34-36(38-40:42-44)in
All round at bust 102(111:121)cm
40(43¾:47½)in
Length to shoulder 63cm/24¾in
Sleeve length 54cm/21¼in

## TENSION

28 sts and 36 rows to 10cm/4in square
measured over patt on 3mm (No 11/
US 3) needles.

## ABBREVIATIONS

See page 8.

# CHEVRON LACE SWEATER

### MAIN PART

KNITTED IN ONE PIECE TO ARMHOLES

With 2¼mm (No 13/US 1) circular needle and
M, cast on 264(288. 312) sts. Mark end of cast
on row to denote end of rounds. Taking care
not to twist the work, cont in rounds of K1,
P1 rib until work measures 7cm/2¾in from
beg.
**Next round** K6, [inc in next st, K11] to last 6
sts, inc in next st, K4, leave last st for next
round. 286(312:338) sts.
Change to 3mm (No 11/US 3) circular needle.
Work in patt as follows:
**1st round** With A, ★ sl 1(K instead of sl st from
last round), K2 tog, psso, K2, yf, K1, yf, K2
tog, K2 tog tbl, yf, K1, yf, K2; rep from ★ to
end.
**2nd round** With A, K to last st, leave last st
for next round. (This round and every alt round
will be P row when patt is worked backwards
and forwards).
**3rd round** With A, ★ sl 1, K2 tog, psso, K1,
yf, K2, yf, K2 tog, K2 tog tbl, yf, K2, yf, K1;
rep from ★ to end.
**4th round** With B, K to last st, leave last st
for next round.
**5th round** With B, ★ sl 1, K2 tog, psso, yf,
K3, yf, K2 tog, K2 tog tbl, yf, K3, yf; rep from
★ to end.
**6th round** With B, as 4th round.
**7th to 9th rounds** With C, work 1st to 3rd
rounds.
**10th to 12th rounds** With D, work 4th to 6th
rounds.
**13th to 15th rounds** With E, work 1st to 3rd
rounds.
**16th to 30th rounds** With M, work 4th to 6th
rounds, then work 1st to 6th rounds twice.
These 30 rounds form patt. Cont in patt until
work measures approximately 39cm/15¼in
from beg, ending with a 24th round of patt.

### *Divide work as follows*

**Next row** Sl last 6 sts of last round and first 7 sts
of next row onto a safety pin, rejoin yarn and
patt 130(143:156) sts for Back, turn.
★★ Work backwards and forwards on this set
of sts only.

**Next row** Patt to end.
**Next row** K1, K2 tog, patt to last 3 sts, sl 1, K1, psso, K1.
Rep last 2 rows 4 times more. 120(133:146) sts.★★
Cont without shaping until work measures 63cm/24¾in from beg, ending with a wrong side row. Leave these sts on a spare needle.
With right side facing, sl next 13 sts onto a safety pin, rejoin yarn to rem sts, patt to end for Front. Work as given for Back from ★★ to ★★.
Cont without shaping until work measures 54cm/21¼in from beg, ending with a wrong side row.

### Shape Neck

**Next row** Patt 38(44:50), turn. Work on this set of sts only.
**Next row** Patt to end.
**Next row** Patt to last 3 sts, sl 1, K1, psso, K1.
Rep last 2 rows 7 times more. 30(36:42) sts.
Cont without shaping until work measures same as Back. Leave these sts on spare needle.
With right side facing, sl 44(45:46) centre Front sts onto a holder, rejoin yarn to rem sts and patt to end.
**Next row** Patt to end.
**Next row** K1, K2 tog, patt to end.
Complete to match first side.

### Join Shoulders

With right side facing, graft each shoulder sts together (see diagram page 39), leaving centre 60(61:62) back neck sts on a holder.

### SLEEVES

With set of four 2¼mm (No 13/US 1) needles and M, cast on 64 sts. Mark end of cast on row to denote end of rounds. Taking care not to twist the work, cont in rounds of K1, P1 rib for 9cm/3½in.
**Next round** [Rib 3, inc in next st, rib 4, inc in next st] to last st, leave last st for next round. 78 sts.
Change to set of four 3mm (No 11/US 3) needles.
Work in patt as given for Main Part, inc one st at each end of every foll 4th round until there are 110 sts, then on every foll 6th round until there are 130 sts, working inc sts into patt.
Cont without shaping until work measures approximately 54cm/21¼in from beg, ending with a 15th round of patt.

### Graft Sleeves

With 2¼mm (No 13/US 1) circular needle and right side facing, pick up but do not K 130 sts evenly around armhole edge including sts on a safety pin. Graft sleeve sts together with armhole sts.

### NECKBAND

With set of four 2¼mm (No 13/US 1) needles, M and right side facing, pick up and K 26 sts down left front neck, K across 44(45:46) centre front sts dec 8 sts evenly, pick up and K 26 sts up right front neck and K across 60(61:62) back neck sts dec 10 sts evenly. 138(140:142) sts. Work 12 rounds in K1, P1 rib. Cast off in rib.

### TO COMPLETE

Hand wash in lukewarm water. Pat dry in towel. Stretch out to size and shape and dry flat away from heat or sunlight.

## MATERIALS

11(12) 1oz hanks of Jamiesons Pure
Shetland.
One in each of 3mm (No 11/US 3) and
3¾mm (No 9/US 5) circular needles,
80cm long.
One set of four in each of 3mm (No 11/
US 3) and 3¾mm (No 9/US 5) double
pointed knitting needles.
Cable needle.

## MEASUREMENTS

To fit bust 81-91(97-107)cm
32-36(38-42)in
All round at bust 105(122)cm
41½(48)in
Length to shoulder 59cm/23¼in
Sleeve length 47cm/18½in

## TENSION

28 sts and 34 rows to 10cm/4in square
measured over patt on 3¾mm (No 9/
US 5) needles.

## ABBREVIATIONS

C6-sl next 3 sts onto cable needle and
leave at front, K3, then K3 from cable
needle
Also see page 8.

# SHETLAND
# LACE
# SWEATER
# WITH
# CABLES

—-=-—

## MAIN PART

KNITTED IN ONE PIECE TO ARMHOLES

With 3mm (No 11/US 3) circular needle cast on 272(314) sts. Mark end of cast on row to denote end of rounds. Taking care not to twist the work, cont in rounds of K1, P1 rib until work measures 7cm/2¾in from beg.

**Next round** ★ Rib 4(3), [inc in next st, rib 10] 12(14) times; rep from ★ once more. 296(342) sts.

Change to 3¾mm (No 9/US 5) circular needle. Work in patt as follows:

**1st round** ★ K2 tog tbl, yf, K6, [yf, K2 tog, K2 tog tbl, yf, K1, yf, K2, sl 1, K2 tog, psso, K2, yf, K1, yf, K2 tog, K2 tog tbl, yf, K6] 6(7) times, yf, K2 tog; rep from ★ once more.

**2nd and every alt round** K. (This round and every alt round will be P row when patt is worked backwards and forwards).

**3rd round** ★ K2 tog tbl, yf, K6, [yf, K2 tog, K2 tog tbl, yf, K2, yf, K1, sl 1, K2 tog, psso, K1, yf, K2, yf, K2 tog, K2 tog tbl, yf, K6] 6(7) times, yf, K2 tog; rep from ★ once more.

**5th round** ★ K2 tog tbl, yf, K6, [yf, K2 tog, K2 tog tbl, yf, K3, yf, sl 1, K2 tog, psso, yf, K3, yf, K2 tog, K2 tog tbl, yf, K6] 6(7) times, yf, K2 tog; rep from ★ once more.

**7th round** ★ K2 tog tbl, yf, C6, [yf, K2 tog, K2 tog tbl, yf, K1, yf, K2, sl 1, K2 tog, psso, K2, yf, K1, yf, K2 tog, K2 tog tbl, yf, C6] 6(7) times, yf, K2 tog; rep from ★ once more.

**9th round** As 3rd round.

**11th round** As 5th round.

**13th round** As 1st round.

**15th round** As 3rd round.

**17th round** ★ K2 tog tbl, yf, C6, [yf, K2 tog, K2 tog tbl, yf, K3, yf, sl 1, K2 tog, psso, yf, K3, yf, K2 tog, K2 tog tbl, yf, C6] 6(7) times, yf, K2 tog; rep from ★ once more.

**19th round** As 1st round.

**21st round** As 3rd round.

**23rd round** As 5th round.

**25th round** As 1st round.

**27th round** *K2 tog tbl, yf, C6, [yf, K2 tog, K2 tog tbl, yf, K2, yf, K1, sl 1, K2 tog, psso, K1, yf, K2, yf, K2 tog, K2 tog tbl, yf, C6] 6(7) times, yf, K2 tog; rep from * once more.
**29th round** As 5th round.
**30th round** K.
These 30 rounds form patt. Cont in patt until work measures approximately 37cm/14½in from beg, ending with a 12th round of patt.

### Divide work as follows
**Next row** Sl last 6(8) sts of last round and 6(8) sts of next row onto a safety pin, rejoin yarn and patt 136(155) sts for Back, turn.
** Work backwards and forwards on Back sts only.
**Next row** Patt to end.
**Next row** K1, sl 1, K1, psso, patt to last 3 sts, K2 tog, K1.
Rep last 2 rows 4(6) times more. 126(141) sts.**
Cont without shaping until work measures 59cm/23¼in from beg, ending with a wrong side row. Leave these sts on a spare needle.
With right side facing, sl next 12(16) sts onto a safety pin, rejoin yarn to rem sts and patt to end for Front. Work as given for Back from ** to **.
Cont without shaping until work measures 54cm/21¼in from beg, ending with a wrong side row.

### Shape Neck
**Next row** Patt 39(46), turn. Work on this set of sts only.
Dec one st at neck edge on every alt row until 34(41) sts rem.
Cont without shaping until work measures same as Back. Leave these sts on a spare needle.
With right side facing, slip 48(49) centre Front

sts onto a holder, rejoin yarn to rem sts and patt to end. Complete to match first side.

### Join Shoulders
With right side facing, graft each shoulder sts together (see diagram page 39), leaving centre 58(59) back neck sts on a holder.

### SLEEVES
With set of four 3mm (No 11/US 3) needles cast on 66 sts. Mark end of cast on row to denote end of rounds. Taking care not to twist the work, cont in rounds of K1, P1 rib until work measures 9cm/3½in from beg.
**Next round** Inc in next st, [rib 1, inc in next st, rib 2, inc in next st] to end. 93 sts.
Change to set of four 3¾mm (No 9/US 5) needles. Work in patt as follows:
**1st round** K2 tog, K2, yf, K1, yf, K2 tog, K2 tog tbl, yf, [K6, yf, K2 tog, K2 tog tbl, yf, K1, yf, K2, sl 1, K2 tog, psso, K2, yf, K1, yf, K2 tog, K2 tog tbl, yf] 3 times, K6, yf, K2 tog, K2 tog tbl, yf, K1, yf, K2, sl 1, K1, psso.
**2nd round** K.
These 2 rounds set position of patt. Cont in patt as set matching patt to Main Part, **at the same time**, inc one st at each end of every 6th round until there are 125 sts, working inc sts into patt.
Cont without shaping until work measures approximately 47cm/18½in from beg, ending with a 12th round of patt.

### Graft Sleeves
With 3mm (No 11/US 3) circular needle and right side facing, pick up but do not K 125 sts evenly around armhole edge, including sts on a safety pin. Graft sleeve sts together with armhole sts.

### NECKBAND
With set of four 3mm (No 11/US 3) needles and right side facing, pick up and K18 sts down left front neck, K across 48(49) centre front sts dec 2 sts evenly, pick up and K18 sts up right front neck, K across 58(59) back neck sts dec 4 sts evenly. 136(138) sts.
Work 16 rounds in K1, P1 rib. Cast off in rib.

### TO COMPLETE
Hand wash in lukewarm water. Pat dry in towel. Stretch out to size and shape and dry flat away from heat or sunlight.

## MATERIALS

One×500g cone of Cambrian Factory Welsh Knitting Wool (knits as DK).
1 pair of 4mm (No 8/US 5) knitting needles.
One 4mm (No 8/US 5) circular needle, 100cm long.
Cable needle.
10(11) buttons.

## MEASUREMENTS

To fit bust 81-91(97-107)cm
32-36(38-42)in
All round at bust 102(118)cm
40(46½)in
Length to shoulder 66(70)cm
26(27½)in
Sleeve seam 40(44)cm/15¾(17¼)in

## TENSION

24 sts and 30 rows to 10cm/4in square measured over patt on 4mm (No 8/ US 5) needles.

## ABBREVIATIONS

C4B-sl next 2 sts onto cable needle and leave at back, K2, then K2 from cable needle.
C4F-sl next 2 sts onto cable needle and leave at front, K2, then K2 from cable needle.
Also see page 8.

# LACE AND CABLE CARDIGAN

-◊-

## MAIN PART
### KNITTED IN ONE PIECE TO ARMHOLES

With 4mm (No 8/US 5) circular needle cast on 239(275) sts.
Work backwards and forwards in welt patt as follows:
**1st row (right side)** P1, [K1, yf, K2 tog, P1] to last 2 sts, K1, P1.
**2nd row** K1, [P1, yrn, P2 tog, K1] to last 2 sts, P1, K1.
Rep these 2 rows 3 times more. ★★ P 2 rows.
Work border patt as follows:
**1st row (right side)** K5, [P1, K5] to end.
**2nd row** K1, P3, K1, [P1, K1, P3, K1] to end.
**3rd row** [K1, P1] twice, [K3, P1, K1, P1] to last st, K1.
**4th row** P2, K1, [P5, K1] to last 2 sts, P2.
K 2 rows inc one st at each end of last row on 2nd size only. 239(277) sts.
Work in main patt as follows:
**1st row (right side)** P2, ★ K4, P1(2), K1, yf, K2, sl 1, K 2 tog, psso, K2, yf, K1, P1(2), K4, P1(2), K1, yf, K2 tog, P1(2); rep from ★ to last 21(23) sts, K4, P1(2), K1, yf, K2, sl 1, K2 tog, psso, K2, yf, K1, P1(2), K4, P2.
**2nd and every foll alt row** K2, ★ P4, K1(2), P9, K1(2), P4, K1(2), P3, K1(2); rep from ★ to last 21(23) sts, P4, K1(2), P9, K1(2), P4, K2.
**3rd row** P2, ★ K4, P1(2), K2, yf, K1, sl 1, K2 tog, psso, K1, yf, K2, P1(2), K4, P1(2), K1, yf, K2 tog, P1(2); rep from ★ to last 21(23) sts, K4, P1(2), K2, yf, K1, sl 1, K2 tog, psso, K1, yf, K2, P1(2), K4, P2.
**5th row** P2, ★ C4B, P1(2), K3, yf, sl 1, K2 tog, psso, yf, K3, P1(2), C4F, P1(2), K1, yf, K2 tog, P1(2); rep from ★ to last 21(23) sts, C4B, P1(2), K3, yf, sl 1, K2 tog, psso, yf, K3, P1(2), C4F, P2.
**6th row** As 2nd row.
These 6 rows form main patt. Cont in main patt until work measures 46(48)cm/18(19)in from beg, ending with a 5th patt row.

### Shape Armholes
**Next row** Patt 55(64), cast off next 9 sts, patt to last 64(73) sts, cast off next 9 sts, patt to end.

Work on last set of 55(64) sts for Right Front. Cont without shaping until work measures 62(66)cm/24½(26)in from beg, ending with a 6th patt row.

### Shape Neck

Cast off 7(8) sts at beg of next row and 2 foll alt rows, then 2 sts at beg of foll 2 alt rows. 30 (36) sts.
Cont without shaping for a few rows until work measures 66(70)cm/26(27½)in from beg, ending with a 6th patt row. Cast off.
With right side facing, rejoin yarn to centre 111(131) sts for Back.
Cont without shaping until work measures 6 rows less than Right Front to cast off edge, ending with a 6th patt row.

### Shape Neck

**Next row** Patt 36(42), turn. Work on this set of sts only. Cast off 3 sts at beg of next and foll alt row. 30(36) sts. Patt 2 rows straight. Cast off.
With right side facing, rejoin yarn to rem Back sts, cast off centre 39(47) sts, patt to end. Patt 1 row. Cast off 3 sts at beg of next and foll alt row. 30(36) sts. Patt 1 row straight. Cast off.
With right side facing, rejoin yarn to rem 55(64) sts for Left Front, patt to end.
Complete to match Right Front, reversing neck shaping.

### SLEEVES

With 4mm (No 8/US 5) needles cast on 47(51) sts. Work as given for Main Part to **. P 2 rows inc one st at each end of last row on 2nd size only. 47(53) sts.
Now work the 4 border patt rows as given for Main Part. K 2 rows.
Work in main patt as given for Main Part, **at the same time**, inc one st at each end of next and 10 foll alt rows, then on every foll 4th row until there are 103(111) sts, working inc sts into patt.
Cont without shaping until work measures 42(46)cm/16½(18)in from beg, ending with a 6th patt row. Cast off.

### BUTTONHOLE BAND

With 4mm (No 8/US 5) needles and right side facing, pick up and K147(163) sts along front edge of Right Front. Beg with a 2nd row, work in welt patt as given for Main Part for 3 rows.
**1st buttonhole row** [Patt 6, cast off 2, then sl st used in casting off back onto left-hand needle, K2 tog, patt 6] to last 3 sts, patt 3.
**2nd buttonhole row** Patt 3, [patt 6, work twice in next st, then cast on 2 sts, patt 6] to end. Patt 2 rows more. Cast off.

### BUTTON BAND

Work to match Buttonhole Band omitting buttonholes.

### NECKBAND

Join shoulder seams.
With 4mm (No 8/US 5) needles and right side facing, pick up and K36(38) sts up right front neck, 6 sts down right back neck, 39(47) sts across centre back neck, 6 sts up left back neck and 36(38) sts down left front neck. 123(135) sts.
Beg with a 2nd row, work in welt patt as given for Main Part for 3 rows.
**1st buttonhole row** Patt 4, cast off 2, then sl st used in casting off back onto left-hand needle, K2 tog, patt to end.
**2nd buttonhole row** Patt to last 5 sts, work twice in next st, then cast on 2 sts, patt 4. Patt 2 rows more. Cast off.

### TO MAKE UP

Sew in sleeves, placing centre of sleeves to shoulder seams and sewing last 6 row ends of sleeve tops to cast off sts at armholes. Join sleeve seams. Sew on buttons.

# HEBRIDEAN GANSEY

--◦◆◦--

## MATERIALS

27(28:30) 25g hanks of Rowan Pure
New Wool DK.
1 pair of 2¼mm (No 13/US 1) knitting
needles.
One in each of 2¼mm (No 13/US 1)
and 3mm (No 11/US 3) circular
needles, 80cm long.
Set of four in each of 2¼mm
(No 13/US 1) and 3mm (No 11/US 3)
double pointed knitting needles.
Cable needle.
2 buttons.

## MEASUREMENTS

To fit bust
81–87(91–97:102–107)cm
32–34(36–38:40–42)in
All round at bust 105(113:121)cm
41½(44½:47½)in
Length to shoulder 69cm/27in
Sleeve seam 52cm/20½in

## TENSION

29 sts and 39 rows to 10cm/4in square
measured over st st on 3mm (No 11/
US 3) needles.

## ABBREVIATIONS

See page 8.

### PANEL A

WORKED OVER 11 STS

**1st round** K7, [P1, K1] twice.
**2nd round** K6, P1, K1, P1, K2.
**3rd round** K5, P1, K1, P1, K3.
**4th round** K4, P1, K1, P1, K4.
**5th round** K3, P1, K1, P1, K5.
**6th round** K2, P1, K1, P1, K6.
**7th round** [K1, P1] twice, K7.
**8th round** As 6th round.
**9th round** As 5th round.
**10th round** As 4th round.
**11th round** As 3rd round.
**12th round** As 2nd round.
These 12 rounds form patt.

### PANEL B

WORKED OVER 9 STS

**1st round** K7, P2.
**2nd round** K6, P3.
**3rd round** K5, P4.
**4th round** K4, P5.
**5th round** K3, P6.
**6th round** K2, P7.
**7th round** K1, P7.
These 7 rounds form patt.

### PANEL C

WORKED OVER 10 STS

**1st row (right side)** P2, K6, P2.
**2nd row** K2, P6, K2.
**3rd to 6th rows** Rep 1st and 2nd rows twice.
**7th row** P2, sl next 3 sts onto cable needle and
leave at back, K3, then K3 from cable needle,
P2.
**8th row** As 2nd row.
These 8 rows form patt.

### PANEL D

WORKED OVER 21(23:21) STS

**1st row (right side)** K21(23:21).
**2nd row** P9(10:9), K3, P9(10:9).
**3rd row** K8(9:8), P5, K8(9:8).
**4th row** P7(8:7), K2, P1, K1, P1, K2, P7(8:7).
**5th row** K6(7:6), P2, K2, P1, K2, P2, K6(7:6).
**6th row** P5(6:5), K2, P2, K3, P2, K2, P5(6:5).
**7th row** K4(5:4), P2, K2, P5, K2, P2, K4(5:4).
**8th row** P3(4:3), K2, P2, K2, P1, K1, P1, K2,
P2, K2, P3(4:3).
**9th row** K2(3:2), [P2, K2] twice, P1, [K2, P2]

twice, K2(3:2).

**10th row** P1(2:1), [K2, P2] twice, K3, [P2, K2] twice, P1(2:1).

**11th row** As 7th row.

**12th row** As 8th row.

**13th row** As 9th row.

**14th row** As 6th row.

**15th row** As 7th row.

**16th row** As 8th row.

**17th row** As 5th row.

**18th row** As 6th row.

**19th row** As 7th row.

**20th row** As 4th row.

**21st row** As 5th row.

**22nd row** As 6th row.

**23rd row** As 3rd row.

**24th row** As 4th row.

**25th row** K7(8:7), [P1, K2] 3 times, K5(6:5).

**26th row** As 2nd row.

**27th row** K9(10:9), P1, K1, P1, K9(10:9).

**28th row** P9(10:9), K1, P1, K1, P9(10:9).

**29th row** K10(11:10), P1, K10(11:10).

**30th and 31st rows** P21(23:21).

**32nd row** K21(23:21).

**33rd row** P21(23:21).
**34th row** K21(23:21).
These 34 rows form patt.

### PANEL E
WORKED OVER 11 STS

**1st row (right side)** K1, yf, K3, sl 1, K2 tog, psso, K3, yf, K1.
**2nd and every foll alt row** P.
**3rd row** K2, yf, K2, sl 1, K2 tog, psso, K2, yf, K2.
**5th row** K3, yf, K1, sl 1, K2 tog, psso, K1, yf, K3.
**7th row** K4, yf, sl 1, K2 tog, psso, yf, K4.
**8th row** P.
These 8 rows form patt.

### MAIN PART
WORKED IN ONE PIECE TO ARMHOLES

**Split welt** With 2¼mm (No 13/US 1) needles and using two strands of yarn, cast on 142(154:164) sts. Using one strand of yarn throughout, work 26 rows in K1 tbl, P1 rib. Leave these sts on a spare needle. Work another piece in same way.
**Next round** With 2¼mm (No 13/US 1) circular needle, ★ rib 8(9:12), [inc in next st, rib 13(14:13) sts] 9(9:10) times, inc in next st, rib 7(9:11) ★ across first piece, then rep from ★ to ★ across second piece. 304(328:350) sts.
Mark end of last round to denote end of rounds. Change to 3mm (No 11/US 3) circular needle. Work in rounds and patt as follows:

#### 1st and 3rd sizes only
**1st round** ★ K1, P1, work 1st row of Panel A, [P1, K1, P1, work 1st row of Panel B, then Panel A] 6(7) times, P1; rep from ★ once more.

#### 2nd size only
**1st round** ★ K1, P1, [work 1st row of Panel A, P1, K1, P1, work 1st row of Panel B] 7 times, P1; rep from ★ once more.

#### All sizes
This round sets patt. Cont in patt, working appropriate rows of Panels until work measures 35cm/13¾in from beg.

#### Shape Gussets
**Next round** ★ M1, K1, m1, patt 151(163:174); rep from ★ once more.
**Next round** ★ K1, m1, K1, m1, K1, patt 151(163:174); rep from ★ once more.

**Next round** ★ K5, patt 151(163:174); rep from ★ once more.
**Next round** ★ K1, m1, K3, m1, K1, patt 151(163:174); rep from ★ once more.
**Next round** ★ K7, patt 151(163:174); rep from ★ once more.
**Next round** ★ K1, m1, K5, m1, K1, patt 151(163:174); rep from ★ once more.
Cont in this way, inc one st at each side of each gusset on every alt round until the round: ★ K27, patt 151(163:174); rep from ★ once more; has been worked.
**Next 4 rounds** ★ With two of set of four 3mm (No 11/US 2) needles, K27, change to 2¼mm (No 13/US 0) circular needle, P151(163:174) sts; rep from ★ once more, inc 2(0:3) sts evenly across each set of P sts on last round. 360(380:408) sts.

#### Divide work as follows

#### 1st and 2nd sizes only
**Next row** Sl last (P) st of last round and first 28 sts of next row onto a holder, rejoin yarn to rem sts, ★★ with 3mm (No 11/US 3) circular needle, work 1st row of Panel C and Panel D, ★ P1(2), work 1st row of Panel E, Panel C and Panel E, P1(2), work 1st row of Panel D; rep from ★ once more, work 1st row of Panel C, turn. 151(161) sts. Work backwards and forwards on this set of sts only for Back.
**Next row** Work 2nd row of Panel C and Panel D, ★ K1(2), work 2nd row of Panel E, Panel C and Panel E, K1(2), work 2nd row of Panel D; rep from ★ once more, work 2nd row of Panel C.
**Next row** Work 3rd row of Panel C and Panel D, ★ P1(2), work 3rd row of Panel E, Panel C and Panel E, P1(2), work 3rd row of Panel D; rep from ★ once more, work 3rd row of Panel C.

#### 3rd size only
**Next row** Sl last (P) st of last round and first 28 sts of next row onto a holder, rejoin yarn to rem sts, ★★ with 3mm (No 11/US 3) circular needle, work 1st row of Panel C, ★ work 1st row of Panel E, P1, work 1st row of Panel D, P1, work 1st row of Panel E and Panel C; rep from ★ twice more, turn. 175 sts. Work backwards and forwards on this set of sts only for Back.
**Next row** Work 2nd row of Panel C, ★ work 2nd row of Panel E, K1, work 2nd row of Panel D, K1, work 2nd row of Panel E and Panel C; rep from ★ twice more.
**Next row** Work 3rd row of Panel C, ★ work

3rd row of Panel E, P1, work 3rd row of Panel D, P1, work 3rd row of Panel E and C; rep from * twice more.

**All sizes**

The last 2 rows set yoke patt. Cont in yoke patt, working appropriate rows of Panels until work measures 66cm/26in from beg, ending with 30th row of Panel D. **

Change to 2¼mm (No 13/US 1) needles. P 1 row. K 1 row. P 1 row. K 1 row. Leave these sts on a spare needle.

With right side facing, sl next 29 sts onto a holder, rejoin yarn to rem sts and work as given for Back from ** to **.

### Shape Neck

Change to 2¼mm (No 13/US 1) needles.

**Next row** P51(54:60), turn. Work on this set of sts only for shoulder gusset.

K 1 row. P 1 row. K 2 rows. P 1 row. K 1 row. P 2 rows. Rep last 8 rows 3 times more, then work first 6 rows again. Leave these sts on a spare needle.

With right side facing, sl 49 (53:55) centre Front sts onto a holder, rejoin yarn to rem 51(54:60) sts and P to end. Complete as given for first side.

### Graft Shoulders

With right side facing, graft shoulder sts together (see diagram page 00), leaving centre 49(53:55) back neck sts on a holder.

### SLEEVES

With set of four 3mm (No 11/US 3) needles, one strand of yarn and right side facing, P1, K27, P1 across one underarm gusset, pick up

an K 140 sts evenly around armhole edge. 169 sts.

Mark end of last round to denote end of rounds. Work in rounds as follows:

**Next round** P1, K1, sl 1, K1, psso, K21, K2 tog, K1, P1, K to end.

**Next round** P1, K25, P1, K to end.

**Next round** P1, K1, sl 1, K1, psso, K19, K2 tog, K1, P1, K to end.

**Next round** P1, K23, P1, K to end.

Cont in this way, dec one st at each side of gusset on next and every alt round until the round: P1, K1, sl 1, K1, psso, K1, K2 tog, K1, P1, K to end; has been worked.

**Next round** P1, K1, sl 1, K2 tog, psso, K1, P1, K to end.

**Next round** P1, yb, sl 1, K2 tog, psso, P1, K to end.

**Next 3 rounds** P1, K1, P1, K to end. 143 sts.

**Next round** [P1, K1] twice, K2 tog, K to last 3 sts, K2 tog tbl, K1.

Rep last 4 rounds until 75 sts rem.

**Next round** P1, K1, P1, K to end.

Rep last round until work measures 45/17¾in.

**Next round** P1, K1, P1, [K2 tog, K6] to end. 66 sts.

Change to set of four 2¼mm (No 13/US 1) needles. Work 7cm in K1 tbl, P1 rib.

Using two strands of yarn, cast off in rib.

### NECKBAND

With set of four 2¼mm (No 13/US 1) needles, two strands of yarn, right side facing and beg at centre of left shoulder gusset, pick up and K 8 sts down left front neck, K across 49(53:55) sts at centre front, pick up and K 16 sts up right front neck and down right back neck, K across 49(53:55) sts at back neck, pick up and K 8 sts up left back neck, then cast on 4 sts for under flap, turn. 134(142:146) sts. Work backwards and forwards, work 1 row in P1, K1 tbl rib.

**1st buttonhole row** Rib 3, cast off 2, rib to end.

**2nd buttonhole row** Rib to last 3 sts, cast on 2, rib to end.

Rib 4 rows. Rep the 2 buttonhole rows again. Rib 2 rows. Cast off in rib.

### TO COMPLETE

Sew on buttons to under flap.

# ARAN JACKET WITH BLACKBERRY STITCH

## MATERIALS

13×100g balls of Hayfield Brig Aran.
1 pair in each of 4mm (No 8/US 6) and
4½mm (No 7/US 8) knitting needles.
2 cable needles.
4 buttons.

## MEASUREMENTS

To fit bust
87–107cm/34–42in
All round at bust 124cm/49in
Length to shoulder 66cm/26in
Sleeve seam (with cuff turned back)
42cm/16½in

## TENSION

19 sts and 25 rows to 10cm/4in square
measured over st st on 4½mm (No 7/
US 8) needles.

## ABBREVIATIONS

C2B–sl next st onto cable needle and
leave at back, K1, then K1 from cable
needle.
C2F–sl next st onto cable needle and
leave at front, K1, then K1 from cable
needle.
C3–sl next st onto 1st cable needle and
leave at front, sl next st onto 2nd cable
needle and leave at back, K1, then K1
from 2nd cable needle, then K1 from
1st cable needle.
Cr3R–sl next st onto cable needle and
leave at back, K2, then K1 from cable
needle.
Cr3L–sl next 2 sts onto cable needle and
leave at front, K1, then K2 from cable
needle.
Cr2L–sl next st onto cable needle and
leave at front, P1, then K1 from cable
needle.
Cr2R–sl next st onto cable needle and
leave at back, K1, then P1 from cable
needle.
Also see page 8.

## PANEL A
WORKED OVER 6 STS

**1st row (right side)** P1, C2B, C2F, P1.
**2nd row** K1, P4, K1.
**3rd row** P1, C2F, C2B, P1.
**4th row** K1, P4, K1.
These 4 rows form patt.

## PANEL B
WORKED OVER 39 STS

**1st row (right side)** P4, C3, P10, sl next 2 sts
onto 1st cable needle and leave at front, sl next
st onto 2nd cable needle and leave at back, K2,
then K1 from 2nd cable needle, then K2 from
1st cable needle, P10, C3, P4.
**2nd row** K4, P3, K10, P5, K10, P3, K4.
**3rd row** P3, C2B, K1, C2F, P8, Cr3R, K1,
Cr3L, P8, C2B, K1, C2F, P3.
**4th row** K3, P5, K8, P7, K8, P5, K3.
**5th row** P2, ★ C2B, K1, yf, sl 1, K1, psso, C2F ★;
P6, Cr3R, K1, yf, sl 1, K1, psso, Cr3L, P6, rep
from ★ to ★ once, P2.
**6th row** K2, P7, K6, P9, K6, P7, K2.
**7th row** P1, ★ C2B, K2 tog, yf, K1, yf, sl 1,
K1, psso, C2F ★; P4, Cr3R, K2 tog, yf, K1,
yf, sl 1, K1, psso, Cr3L, P4, rep from ★ to ★
once, P1.
**8th row** K1, P9, K4, P11, K4, P9, K1.
**9th row** P1, Cr2L, K5, Cr2R, P3, Cr3R, K2
tog, yf, K3, yf, sl 1, K1, psso, Cr3L, P3, Cr2L,
K5, Cr2R, P1.
**10th row** K2, P7, K4, P13, K4, P7, K2.
**11th row** P2, Cr2L, K3, Cr2R, P3, Cr3R, K2
tog, yf, K5, yf, sl 1, K1, psso, Cr3L, P3, Cr2L,
K3, Cr2R, P2.
**12th row** K3, P5, K4, P15, K4, P5, K3.
**13th row** P3, Cr2L, K1, Cr2R, P3, Cr3R, K2
tog, yf, K7, yf, sl 1, K1, psso, Cr3L, P3, Cr2L,
K1, Cr2R, P3.
**14th row** K4, P3, K4, P17, K4, P3, K4.
These 14 rows from patt.

## BACK

With 4½mm (No 7/US 8) needles cast on 134 sts. Work border patt as follows:

**1st row (right side)** P.

**2nd row** P1, ★ [K1, P1, K1] all in next st, P3 tog; rep from ★ to last st, P1.

**3rd row** P.

**4th row** P1, ★ P3 tog, [K1, P1, K1] all in next st; rep from ★ to last st, P1.

These 4 rows form border patt. Rep these 4 rows twice more, then work 1st to 3rd rows again. ★★

**Next row** [P1, K1] 7 times, ★ P4, K5, P3, K10, P2, m1, P2, K10, P3, K5, P4 ★; [K1, P1] twice, K1, m1, K1, [P1, K1] twice, rep from ★ to ★ once, [K1, P1] 7 times. 137 sts.

Work in main patt as follows:

**1st row (right side)** P1, [K1, P1] 6 times, work 1st row of Panel A, Panel B and Panel A, P1, [K1, P1] 4 times, work 1st row of Panel A, Panel B and Panel A, P1, [K1, P1] 6 times.

This row sets main patt. Cont in main patt, working appropriate rows of Panels until work measures approximately 64cm/25¼in from beg, ending with 8th row of Panel B.

### Shape Neck

**Next row** Patt 55, turn. Work on this set of sts only.

Keeping patt correct, dec one st at neck edge on next 6 rows. Cast off rem 49 sts.

With right side facing, rejoin yarn to rem sts, cast off centre 27 sts, patt to end. Complete to match first side.

## POCKET LININGS

MAKE 2

With 4mm (No 8/US 6) needles cast on 29 sts. Beg with a K row, work 43 rows in st st. Leave these sts on a holder.

## LEFT FRONT

With 4½mm (No 7/US 8) needles cast on 74 sts. Work as give for Back to ★★.

**Next row** P1, ★ P3 tog, [K1, P1, K1] all in next st; rep from ★ twice more and slip these 13 sts onto a holder, work on rem sts as follows: K1, P4, K5, P1, m1, P1, K10, P2, m1, P2, K10, P1, m1, P1, K5, P4, [K1, P1] 7 times. 64 sts.

Work in main patt as follows:

**1st row (right side)** P1, [K1, P1] 6 times, work

1st row of Panel A, Panel B and Panel A.

**2nd row** Work 2nd row of Panel A, Panel B and Panel A, P1, [K1, P1] 6 times.

These 2 rows set main patt. Cont in main patt, working appropriate rows of Panels until 44 rows of main patt in all have been worked.

### Place Pocket

**Next row** Patt 24, slip next 29 sts onto a holder, patt across sts of one pocket lining, patt to end. Cont in main patt across all sts until work measures 39cm/15¼in from beg, ending with a wrong side row.

### Shape Front

Keeping patt correct, dec one st at end (front edge) of next row and every foll 4th row until 49 sts rem.

Cont without shaping until work measures same as Back to cast off edge, ending with a right side row. Cast off.

## RIGHT FRONT

With 4½mm (No 7/US 8) needles cast on 74 sts. Work as given for Back to ★★.

**Next row** [P1, K1] 7 times, P4, K5, P1, m1, P1, K10, P2, m1, P2, K10, P1, m1, P1, K5, P4, K1, turn; leaving rem 13 sts on a holder. 64 sts.

Work in main patt as follows:

**1st row (right side)** Work 1st row of Panel A, Panel B and Panel A, P1, [K1, P1] 6 times.

**2nd row** P1, [K1, P1] 6 times, work 2nd row of Panel A, Panel B and Panel A.

These 2 rows set main patt. Cont in main patt, working appropriate rows of Panels until 44 rows of main patt in all have been worked.

### Place Pocket

**Next row** Patt 11, slip next 29 sts onto a holder, patt across sts of one pocket lining, patt to end. Complete to match Left Front, reversing front shaping.

## SLEEVES

With 4½mm (No 7/US 8) needles cast on 58 sts. Work 30 rows of border patt as given for Back.

**Next row** P29, m1, P29. 59 sts.

**Next row** K1, [P1, K1] twice, P4, K5, P3, K10, P5, K10, P3, K5, P4, K1, [P1, K1] twice.

Work in main patt as follows:

**1st row (right side)** [K1, P1] twice, work 1st

row of Panel A, Panel B and Panel A, [P1, K1] twice.

This row sets main patt. Cont in main patt, working appropriate rows of Panels, **at the same time**, inc one st at each end of next and 4 foll alt rows, then on every foll 4th row until there are 107 sts, working inc sts into side edge patt.

Cont without shaping until work measures approximately 47cm/18½in from beg, ending with a 1st row of Panel B. Cast off.

### BUTTON BAND

Join shoulder seams.

With 4½mm (No 7/US 8) needles, rejoin yarn at inner edge to sts on Left Front holder, cast on 1 st, border patt to end. 14 sts.

Cont in border patt until band when slightly stretched, fits up Left Front to centre back neck, ending with a right side row. Leave these sts on a holder. Sew band in place. Mark button positions, first one to come in line with beg of main patt and last one in line with beg of front shaping and rem 2 evenly spaced between.

### BUTTONHOLE BAND

Work to match Button Band making button-holes at markers as follows:

**1st buttonhole row (right side)** Patt 5, cast off 4, patt to end.

**2nd buttonhole row** Patt 5, cast on 4, patt to end.

With right sides of bands together, cast off together 14 sts (see diagram page 39). Sew band in position.

### POCKET TOPS

With 4½mm (No 7/US 8) needles and right side facing, work across sts of one pocket top as follows: P14, P twice in next st, P14. 30 sts.

Beg with a 2nd row, work 11 rows in border patt as given for Back. Cast off purlwise.

### TO MAKE UP

Catch down pocket linings and sides of pocket tops. Sew on sleeves, placing centre of sleeves to shoulder seams. Join side and sleeve seams. Sew on buttons.

## MATERIALS

12(13:13) 100g balls of Hayfield Brig
Aran.
1 pair in each of 4mm (No 8/US 5) and
5mm (No 6/US 7) knitting needles.
Cable needle.

## MEASUREMENTS

To fit bust 86(91:97)cm/34(36:38)in
All round at bust 108(115:121)cm
42½(45¼:47½)in
Length to shoulder 68(69:70)cm
26¾(27:27½)in
Sleeve seam 40(41:42)cm
15¾(16:16½)in

## TENSION

24 sts and 24 rows to 10cm/4in square
measured over patt on 5mm (No 6/
US 7) needles.

## ABBREVIATIONS

C8B-sl next 4 sts onto cable needle and
leave at back, K4, then K4 from cable
needle.
C8F-sl next 4 sts onto cable needle and
leave at front, K4, then K4 from cable
needle.
C2B-sl next st onto cable needle and
leave at back, K1, then K1 from cable
needle.
C2F-sl next st onto cable needle and
leave at front, K1, then K1 from cable
needle.
Cr2R-sl next st onto cable needle and
leave at back, K1, then P1 from cable
needle.
Cr2L-sl next st onto cable needle and
leave at front, P1, then K1 from cable
needle.
Cr3R-sl next st onto cable needle and
leave at back, K2, then P1 from cable
needle.
Cr3L-sl next 2 sts onto cable needle and
leave at front, P1, then K2 from cable
needle.
Cr5R-sl next 2 sts onto cable needle and
leave at back, K3, then P2 from cable
needle.
Cr5L-sl next 3 sts onto cable needle and
leave at front, P2, then K3 from cable
needle.
MB-make bobble as follows: K into
front, back, front, back and front of
next st, turn, P5, turn, [K5, turn, P5
turn] twice, K5, then pass 2nd, 3rd, 4th
and 5th st over 1st st.
Also see page 8.

# BOBBLE ARAN WITH POLO NECK

## PANEL A

WORKED OVER 16(18:20) STS

**1st row (right side)** P4(5:6), C8B, P4(5:6).
**2nd row** K4(5:6), P8, K4(5:6).
**3rd row** P4(5:6), K8, P4(5:6).
**4th row** As 2nd row.
**5th to 8th rows** Rep 3rd and 4th rows twice.
**9th row** P4(5:6), C8F, P4(5:6).
**10th to 16th rows** Work 2nd to 8th rows.
These 16 rows form patt.

## PANEL B

WORKED OVER 16 STS

**1st row (right side)** P7, K2, P7.
**2nd row** K7, P2, K7.
**3rd row** P6, C2B, C2F, P6.
**4th row** K5, Cr2L, P2, Cr2R, K5.
**5th row** P4, Cr2R, C2B, C2F, Cr2L, P4.
**6th row** K3, Cr2L, K1, P4, K1, Cr2R, K3.
**7th row** P2, Cr2R, P1, Cr2R, K2, Cr2L, P1, Cr2L, P2.
**8th row** K1, Cr2L, K2, P1, K1, P2, K1, P1, K2, Cr2R, K1.
**9th row** Cr2R, P2, Cr2R, P1, K2, P1, Cr2L, P2, Cr2L.
**10th row** P1, K3, P1, K2, P2, K2, P1, K3, P1.
**11th row** MB, P2, Cr2R, P2, K2, P2, Cr2L, P2, MB.
**12th row** K3, P1, K3, P2, K3, P1, K3.
**13th row** P3, MB, P3, K2, P3, MB, P3.
**14th row** As 2nd row.
**15th and 16th rows** As 1st and 2nd rows.
These 16 rows form patt.

## PANEL C

WORKED OVER 16(18:20) STS

**1st row (right side)** P4(5:6), C8B, P4(5:6).
**2nd row** K4(5:6), P8, K4(5:6).
**3rd row** P4(5:6), K8, P4(5:6).
**4th row** As 2nd row.
**5th to 8th rows** Rep 3rd and 4th rows twice.
These 8 rows form patt.

## PANEL D

### WORKED OVER 32 STS.

**1st row (right side)** MB, P2, K2, P8, sl next 3 sts onto cable needle and leave at back, K3, then K3 from cable needle, P8, K2, P2, MB.

**2nd row** K3, P2, K8, P6, K8, P2, K3.

**3rd row** P2, Cr3R, P6, Cr5R, Cr5L, P6, Cr3L, P2.

**4th row** K2, P2, K7, P3, K4, P3, K7, P2, K2.

**5th row** P1, Cr3R, P5, Cr5R, P4, Cr5L, P5, Cr3L, P1.

**6th row** K1, P2, K6, P3, K8, P3, K6, P2, K1.

**7th row** Cr3R, P6, K3, P8, K3, P6, Cr3L.

**8th row** P2, K7, P3, K8, P3, K7, P2.

**9th row** K2, P2, MB, P4, K3, P8, K3, P4, MB, P2, K2.

**10th row** As 8th row.

**11th row** Cr3L, P6, K3, P8, K3, P6, Cr3R.

**12th row** As 6th row.

**13th row** P1, Cr3L, P5, Cr5L, P4, Cr5R, P5, Cr3R, P1.

**14th row** As 4th row.

**15th row** P2, Cr3L, P6, Cr5L, Cr5R, P6, Cr3R, P2.

**16th row** As 2nd row.

These 16 rows form patt.

## PANEL E

### WORKED OVER 16(18:20) STS

Work as given for Panel C, but working C8F instead of C8B.

## PANEL F

### WORKED OVER 16(18:20) STS

Work as given for Panel A, but working C8F instead of C8B and C8B instead of C8F.

## BACK

With 4mm (No 8/US 5) needles cast on 110(114:114) sts.

**1st row (right side)** K2(0:0), [P2, K2] to last 0(2:2) sts, P0(2:2).

**2nd row** P2(0:0), [K2, P2] to last 0(2:2) sts, K0(2:2).

Rep these 2 rows until work measures 7cm/2¾in from beg, ending with a 1st row.

**1st size only**

**Next row** Rib 4, ★ [m1, rib 2] 4 times, rib 20, [m1, rib 2] 4 times ★; rib 10, m1, rib 2, m1, rib 6, m1, rib 2, m1, rib 12, rep from ★ to ★ once, rib 2.

**2nd size only**

**Next row** Rib 8, [m1, rib 2] 3 times, rib 8, m1, rib 2, m1, rib 10, [m1, rib 2] 4 times, rib 4, m1, rib 2, m1, rib 4, m1, rib 10, m1, rib 4, m1, rib 2, m1, rib 6, [m1, rib 2] 4 times, rib 8, m1, rib 2, m1, rib 10, [m1, rib 2] 3 times, rib 6.

**3rd size only**

**Next row** ★ Rib 6, [m1, rib 2] 4 times; rep from ★ twice more, rib 2, [m1, rib 2, m1, rib 6] 3 times, [m1, rib 2] twice, ★★ [rib 2, m1] 4 times, rib 6; rep from ★★ twice more.

**All sizes**

130(138:146) sts.

Change to 5mm (No 6/US 7) needles. Work in patt as follows:

**1st row (right side)** P1, work across 1st row of Panel A, Panel B, Panel C, Panel D, Panel E, Panel B and Panel F, P1.

**2nd row** K1, work across 2nd row of Panel F, Panel B, Panel E, Panel D, Panel C, Panel B and Panel A, K1.

These 2 rows set patt. Cont in patt, working appropriate rows of Panels until work measures 40cm/15¾in from beg, ending with a wrong side row.

### Shape Armholes

Keeping patt correct, cast off 3(4:5) sts at beg of next 2 rows. 124(130:136) sts. ★★★

Cont without shaping until work measures 66(67:68)cm/26(26¼:26¾)in from beg, ending with a wrong side row.

### Shape Neck

**Next row** Patt 45(47:49), turn. Work on this set of sts only.

Dec one st at neck edge on next 2 rows. Patt 3 rows straight. Cast off rem 43(45:47) sts.

With right side facing, slip centre 34(36:38) sts onto a holder, rejoin yarn to rem sts and patt to end. Complete to match first side.

### FRONT

Work as given for Back to ★★★. Cont without shaping until work measures 61(62:63)cm/24(24¼:24¾)in from beg, ending with a wrong side row.

### Shape Neck

**Next row** Patt 56(59:62), turn. Work on this set of sts only.

Keeping patt correct, cast off 3 sts at beg of next and foll alt row, 2 sts at beg of foll 3(3:4) alt rows and 1(2:1) sts at beg of foll alt row. 43(45:47) sts.

Cont without shaping for a few rows until work measures same as Back to cast off edge, ending with a wrong side row. Cast off.

With right side facing, slip centre 12 sts onto a holder, rejoin yarn to rem sts and patt to end. Patt 1 row. Complete to match first side.

### SLEEVES

With 4mm (No 8/US 5) needles cast on 50 sts.
**1st row (right side)** P2, [K2, P2] to end.
**2nd row** K2, [P2, K2] to end.
Rep these 2 rows until work measures 7cm/2¾in from beg, ending with a 1st row.

**1st size only**
**Next row** [Rib 2, m1] 4 times, rib 12, m1, rib 2, m1, rib 6, m1, rib 2, m1, rib 12, [m1, rib 2] 4 times.
**2nd size only**
**Next row** [Rib 2, m1] 4 times, rib 6, [m1, rib 6, m1, rib 2] 3 times, rib 4, [m1, rib 2] 4 times.
**3rd size only**
**Next row** [Rib 2, m1] 4 times, rib 4, [m1, rib 2, m1, rib 6] 3 times, m1, rib 2, m1, rib 4, [m1, rib 2] 4 times.
**All sizes**
62(64:66) sts.
Change to 5mm (No 6/US 7) needles. Work in patt as follows:
**1st row (right side)** P3, C8B, P4(5:6) (part of 1st row of Panel C), work across 1st row of Panel D, P4(5:6), C8F, P3 (part of Panel E).
**2nd row** K3, P8, K4(5:6), work across 2nd row of Panel D, K4(5:6), P8, K3.
These 2 rows set patt. Cont in patt, working appropriate rows of Panels, **at the same time**, inc one st at each end of next and every foll alt row until there are 130(136:140) sts, working inc sts into patt to match Back.
Cont without shaping until work measures 41(42:44)cm/16(16½:17¼)in from beg, ending with a wrong side row. Cast off.

### COLLAR

Join right shoulder seam.
With 4mm (No 8/US 5) needles and right side facing, pick up and K23(24:27) sts down left front neck, K across 12 sts at centre front, pick up and K23 (24:27) sts up right front neck, 9 sts down right back neck, K across 34(36:38) sts at centre back neck, pick up and K9 sts up left back neck. 110(114:122) sts.
Beg with a 2nd row, work in rib as given for Sleeves for 23cm/9in. Cast off in rib.

### TO MAKE UP

Join left shoulder and collar seam, reversing seam on collar on last 13cm/5in.
Sew on sleeves, placing centre of sleeves to shoulder seams and sewing last 1(1.5:2)cm/¼(½:¾)in of row ends on sleeve tops to cast off sts at armholes. Join side and sleeve seams.

## MATERIALS

11(12:13:14) 100g balls of Hayfield Brig
Aran.
1 pair in each of 4mm (No 8/US 6) and
4½mm (No 7/US 8) knitting needles.
Set of four 4mm (No 8/US 6) double
pointed knitting needles.
Cable needle.

## MEASUREMENTS

To fit chest 97(102:107:112)cm
38(40:42:44)in
All round at chest 108(114:118:122)cm
42½(45:46½:48)in
Length to shoulder 71(72:73:74)cm
28(28½:28¾:29¼)in
Sleeve seam 47(48:49:50)cm
18½(19:19¼:19¾)in

## TENSION

19 sts and 25 rows to 10cm/4in square
measured over st st on 4½mm (No 7/
US 8) needles.

## ABBREVIATIONS

C4B-sl next 2 sts onto cable needle and
leave at back, K2, then K2 from cable
needle.
C4F-sl next 2 sts onto cable needle and
leave at front, K2, then K2 from cable
needle.
Cr3R-sl next st onto cable needle and
leave at back, K2, then P1 from cable
needle.
Cr3L-sl next 2 sts onto cable needle and
leave at front, P1, then K2 from cable
needle.
Tw2-K into front of second st then K
into front of first st, slipping both sts
off needle together.
Also see page 8.

# ARAN
# FISHING
# SHIRT

---

### PANEL A
WORKED OVER 8 STS

**1st row (right side)** P2, K4, P2.
**2nd and foll alt row** K2, P4, K2.
**3rd row** As 1st row.
**5th row** P2, sl next 3 sts onto cable needle and leave at back, K1, then [sl first st on cable needle back onto left-hand needle, K this st] 3 times, P2.
**6th row** As 2nd row.
These 6 rows form patt.

### PANEL B
WORKED OVER 17 STS

**1st row (right side)** P1, [K2, P3, K2, P1] twice.
**2nd row** K6, P2, K1, P2, K6.
**3rd row** P6, sl next 3 sts onto cable needle and leave at back, K2, then sl first (P) sts on cable needle back onto left-hand needle, P this st, K2 from cable needle, P6.
**4th row and every foll alt row** K the K sts, P the P sts as they appear.
**5th row** P5, Cr3R, K1, Cr3L, P5.
**7th row** P4, Cr3R, K1, P1, K1, Cr3L, P4.
**9th row** P3, Cr3R, K1, [P1, K1] twice, Cr3L, P3.
**11th row** P2, Cr3R, K1, [P1, K1] 3 times, Cr3L, P2.
**13th row** P1, Cr3R, K1, [P1, K1] 4 times, Cr3L, P1.
**14th row** As 4th row.
These 14 rows form patt.

### PANEL C
WORKED OVER 30 STS

**1st row (right side)** P7, [K4, P2] 3 times, P5.
**2nd row and every foll alt row** K the K sts, P the P sts as they appear.
**3rd row** P6, [Cr3R, Cr3L] 3 times, P6.
**5th row** P5, Cr3R, [P2, C4B] twice, P2, Cr3L, P5.
**7th row** P4, Cr3R, P2, [Cr3R, Cr3L] twice, P2, Cr3L, P4.
**9th row** P3, [Cr3R, P2] twice, C4F, [P2, Cr3L] twice, P3.
**11th row** [P2, Cr3R] 3 times, [Cr3L, P2] 3 times.

**13th row** [P2, K2, P1] 3 times, [P1, K2, P2] 3 times.

**15th row** [P2, Cr3L] 3 times, [Cr3R, P2] 3 times.

**17th row** P3, [Cr3L, P2] twice, C4F, [P2, Cr3R] twice, P3.

**19th row** P4, Cr3L, P2, [Cr3L, Cr3R] twice, P2, Cr3R, P4.

**21st row** P5, Cr3L, [P2, C4B] twice, P2, Cr3R, P5.

**23rd row** P6, [Cr3L, Cr3R] 3 times, P6.

**25th row** P7, [C4F, P2] 3 times, P5.

**26th row** As 2nd row.

These 26 rows form patt.

### BACK AND FRONT
#### ALIKE

With 4mm (No 8/US 6) needles cast on 126(133:140:147) sts.

Work in rib patt as follows:

**1st row (right side)** K1, [P1, K3, P1, Tw2] to last 6 sts, P1, K3, P1, K1.

**2nd row** K1, [K1, P3, K1, P2] to last 6 sts, K1, P3, K2.

These 2 rows form rib patt. Cont in rib patt until work measures 15cm/6in from beg, ending with a wrong side row.

K 1 row inc 10(7:4:1) sts across. 136(140:144: 148) sts. K 1 row. P 1 row. K 1 row.

Change to 4½mm (No 7/US 8) needles. Work in main patt as follows:

**1st row (right side)** K2(0:2:0), [P2, K2] 2(3:3:4) times, ★ K1 tbl, work 1st row of Panel A, K1 tbl, P2, K1 tbl, work 1st row of Panel B, K1 tbl, P2, K1 tbl, work 1st row of Panel A, K1 tbl ★; work 1st row of Panel C, rep from ★ to ★ once, [K2, P2] 2(3:3:4) times, K2(0:2:0).

**2nd row** P2(0:2:0), [K2, P2] 2(3:3:4) times, ★ P1, work 2nd row of Panel A, P1, K2, P1, work 2nd row of Panel B, P1, K2, P1, work 2nd row of Panel A, P1 ★; work 2nd row of Panel C, rep from ★ to ★ once, [P2, K2] 2(3:3:4) times, P2(0:2:0).

**3rd row** P2(0:2:0), [K2, P2] 2(3:3:4) times, ★ K1 tbl, work 3rd row of Panel A, K1 tbl, P2, K1 tbl, work 3rd row of Panel B, K1 tbl, P2, K1 tbl, work 3rd row of Panel A, K1 tbl ★; work 3rd row of Panel C, rep from ★ to ★ once, [P2, K2] 2(3:3:4) times, P2(0:2:0).

**4th row** K2(0:2:0), [P2, K2] 2(3:3:4) times, ★ P1, work 4th row of Panel A, P1, K2, P1, work 4th row of Panel B, P1, K2, P1, work

4th row of Panel A, P1 ★; work 4th row of Panel C, rep from ★ to ★ once, [K2, P2] 2(3:3:4) times, K2(0:2:0).

These 4 rows set patt. Cont in patt as set, working appropriate rows of Panels until work measures 47cm/18½in from beg, ending with a wrong side row.

### Shape Armholes

Keeping patt correct, cast off 10(11:12:13) sts at beg of next 2 rows. 116(118:120:122) sts.

Cont without shaping until work measures 67(68:69:70)cm/26¼(26¾:27:27½)in from beg, ending with a wrong side row.

### Shape Shoulders

Cast off 38(38:39:39) sts at beg of next 2 rows. Leave rem 40(42:42:44) sts on a holder.

### SLEEVES

With 4mm (No 8/US 6) needles cast on 49(56:56:63) sts.

Work in rib patt as given for Back until work measures 7cm/2¾in from beg, ending with a wrong side row.

**Next row** K5(0:1:2), [K twice in next st, K0(2:1:2), K twice in next st, K1] to last 8(1:3:6) sts, [K twice in next st, K3(0:2:2) sts] 2(1:1:2) times. 75(79:83:87) sts.

K 1 row. P 1 row. K 1 row.

Change to 4½mm (No 7/US 8) needles. Work in main patt as follows:

**1st row (right side)** P0(2:0:2), [K2, P2] 4(4:5:5) times, K1 tbl, work 1st row of Panel A, K1 tbl, P2, K1 tbl, work 1st row of Panel B, K1 tbl, P2, K1 tbl, work 1st row of Panel A, K1 tbl, [P2, K2] 4(4:5:5) times, P0(2:0:2).

**2nd row** K0(2:0:2), [P2, K2] 4(4:5:5) times, P1, work 2nd row of Panel A, P1, K2, P1, work 2nd row of Panel B, P1, K2, P1, work 2nd row of Panel A, P1, [K2, P2] 4(4:5:5) times, K 0(2:0:2).

**3rd row** K0(2:0:2), [P2, K2] 4(4:5:5) times, K1 tbl, work 3rd row of Panel A, K1 tbl, P2, K1 tbl, work 3rd row of Panel B, K1 tbl, P2, K1 tbl, work 3rd row of Panel A, K1 tbl, [K2, P2] 4(4:5:5) times, K0(2:0:2).

**4th row** P0(2:0:2), [K2, P2] 4(4:5:5) times, P1, work 4th row of Panel A, P1, K2, P1, work 4th row of Panel B, P1, K2, P1, work 4th row of Panel A, P1, [P2, K2] 4(4:5:5) times, P0(2:0:2).

These 4 rows set patt. Cont in patt as set, working appropriate rows of Panels, **at the same time**, inc one st at each end of next and every foll 6th row until there are 103(107:111:115) sts, working inc sts into side edge patt.

Cont without shaping until work measures 51(52:54:55)cm/20(20½:21¼:21¾)in from beg, ending with a wrong side row.

### Shape Saddle

Keeping patt correct, cast off 40(42:44:46) sts at beg of next 2 rows. Cont without shaping on rem 23 sts until saddle, when slightly stretched, fits across cast off shoulder sts on Back, ending with a wrong side row. Leave these sts on a holder.

## COLLAR

Sew on sleeves, sewing saddles to shoulders on Back and Front and last 4(4:5:5)cm/1½(1½:2:2)in of row ends of sleeve tops to cast off sts at armholes.

With set of four 4mm (No 8/US 6) needles and right side facing, K across sts of left saddle, centre front neck, right saddle and centre back neck. 126(130:130:134) sts. Work in rounds.

P 1 round inc 0(3:3:6) sts. 126(133:133:140) sts. Work in rib patt as follows:

**1st round** [P1, K3, P1, Tw2] to end.
**2nd round** [P1, K3, P1, K2] to end.

Rep these 2 rounds until work measures 10cm/4in. Cast off loosely in rib.

## TO MAKE UP

Join side and sleeve seams.

## MATERIALS

*Round Neck Cardigan* 5(7:12:12:13:14)
100g balls of Hayfield Brig Aran.
7(7:8:8:9:9) buttons.
*V Neck Cardigan* 5(7:12:12:13:14) 100g
balls of Hayfield Brig Aran.
6(6:7:7:7:7) buttons.
1 pair in each of 3¾mm (No 9/US 6)
and 4½mm (No 7/US 8) knitting
needles.
One 3¾mm (No 9/US 6) circular
needle, 100cm long for V Neck
Cardigan.
Cable needle.

## MEASUREMENTS

To fit chest or bust
61-66(71-76:81-86:91-97:102-107:
112-117)cm
24-26(28-30:32-34:36-38:40-42:
44-46)in
All round at chest or bust
81(97:115:121:125:135) cm
32(38:45¼:47½:49¼:53)in
Length to shoulder
42(50:64:65:66:68)cm
16½(19½:25:25½:26:26¾)in
Sleeve seam 27(34:42:44:45:47)cm
10½(13¼:16½:17¼:17¾:18½)in

## TENSION

19 sts and 25 rows to 10cm/4in square
measured over st st on 4½mm (No 7/
US 8) needles.

## ABBREVIATIONS

C4B–sl next 2 sts onto cable needle and
leave at back, K2, then K2 from cable
needle.
C4F–sl next 2 sts onto cable needle and
leave at front, K2, then K2 from cable
needle.
T4B–sl next 2 sts onto cable needle and
leave at back, K2, then P2 from cable
needle.
T4F–sl next 2 sts onto cable needle and
leave at front, P2, then K2 from cable
needle.
Also see page 8.

# FAMILY ARAN CARDIGANS

---◆---

### PANEL A
WORKED OVER 10 STS

**1st row (right side)** P1, K8, P1.
**2nd row** K1, P8, K1.
**3rd and 4th rows** Work 1st and 2nd rows.
**5th row** P1, C4F, C4B, P1.
**6th row** As 2nd row.
These 6 rows form patt.

### PANEL B
WORKED OVER 18 STS

**1st row (right side)** P3, C4F, P4, C4F, P3.
**2nd row** K3, P4, K4, P4, K3.
**3rd row** P3, K4, P4, K4, P3.
**4th row** As 2nd row.
**5th and 6th rows** Work 1st and 2nd rows.
**7th row** P1, [T4B, T4F] twice, P1.
**8th row** K1, P2, K4, P4, K4, P2, K1.
**9th row** P1, K2, P4, C4F, P4, K2, P1.
**10th row** As 8th row.
**11th row** P1, K2, P4, K4, P4, K2, P1.
**12th to 22nd rows** Rep 8th to 11th rows twice,
then work 8th to 10th rows again.
**23rd row** P1, [T4F, T4B] twice, P1.
**24th row** As 2nd row.
These 24 rows form patt.

## ROUND NECK CARDIGAN

### BACK

With 3¾mm (No 9/US 6) needles cast on
71(81:89:97:109:117) sts.
**1st row (right side)** K1, [P1, K1] to end.
**2nd row** P1, [K1, P1] to end.
Rep these 2 rows until work measures 6(6:6:7:
7:7)cm/2½(2½:2½:2¾:2¾:2¾)in from beg,
ending with a right side row.
**Next row** Rib 4(1:1:7:3:3), [inc in each of next
1(1:2:2:1:1) sts, rib 1] to last 3(0:1:6:2:2) sts, rib
3(0:1:6:2:2). 103(121:147:153:161:173) sts.
Change to 4½mm (No 7/US 8) needles. Work
in patt as follows:
**1st row (right side)** P10(19:21:24:17:23), ★ K1
tbl, [work 1st row of Panel A, K1 tbl]
1(1:2:2:3:3) times ★; work 1st row of Panel B,
K1 tbl, [work 1st row of Panel A, K1 tbl] twice,

work 1st row of Panel B, rep from ★ to ★ once, P to end.

**2nd row** K1(2:0:3:0:2), ★ [K1, P1, K1] all in next st, P3 tog ★; rep from ★ to ★ 1(3:4:4:3:4) times more, K1, ★★ P1, [work 2nd row of Panel A, P1] 1(1:2:2:3:3) times ★★; work 2nd row of Panel B, P1, [work 2nd row of Panel A, P1] twice, work 2nd row of Panel B, rep from ★★ to ★★ once, K1, rep from ★ to ★ 2(4:5:5:4:5) times, K1(2:0:3:0:2).

**3rd row** P10(19:21:24:17:23), ★ K1 tbl, [work 3rd row of Panel A, K1 tbl] 1(1:2:2:3:3) times ★; work 3rd row of Panel B, K1 tbl, [work 3rd row of Panel A, K1 tbl] twice, work 3rd row of Panel B, rep from ★ to ★ once, P to end.

**4th row** K1(2:0:3:0:2), ★ P3 tog, [K1, P1, K1] all in next st ★; rep from ★ to ★ 1(3:4:4:3:4) times more, K1, ★★ P1, [work 4th row of Panel A, P1] 1(1:2:2:3:3) times ★★; work 4th row of Panel B, P1, [work 4th row of Panel A, P1] twice, work 4th row of Panel B, rep from ★★ to ★★ once, K1, rep from ★ to ★ 2(4:5:5:4:5) times, K1(2:0:3:0:2).

These 4 rows set patt. Cont in patt as set, working appropriate rows of Panels until work measures 39(47:61:62:63:65)cm/15½(18½:24:24½:25:25½)in from beg, ending with a wrong side row.

### *Shape Shoulders*

Cast off 36(43:53:55:58:63) sts at beg of next 2 rows. Leave rem 31(35:41:43:45:47) sts on a holder.

### POCKET LININGS

MAKE 2

With 4½mm (No 7/US 8) needles cast on 20(20:30:30:30:30) sts. Work in K1, P1 rib for 6(6:8:8:8:8)cm/2½(2½:3:3:3:3)in. Leave these sts on a holder.

### LEFT FRONT

With 3¾mm (No 9/US 6) needles cast on 35(41:45:49:55:59) sts.
Work in rib as given for Back for 6(6:6:7:7:7)cm/2½(2½:2½:2¾:2¾:2¾)in, ending with a right side row.

**Next row** Rib 1(1:1:4:2:2), [inc in each of next 1(1:2:2:1:1) sts, rib 1] to last 2(2:2:6:3:3) sts, inc in each of next 1(1:1:2:1:1) sts, rib 1(1:1:4:2:2). 52(61:74:77:81:87) sts. ★★★
Change to 4½mm (No 7/US 8) needles. Work in patt as follows:

**1st row (right side)** P10(19:21:24:17:23), K1 tbl, [work 1st row of Panel A, K1 tbl] 1(1:2:2:3:3) times, work 1st row of Panel B, K1 tbl, work 1st row of Panel A, P1.

**2nd row** K1, work 2nd row of Panel A, P1, work 2nd row of Panel B, P1, [work 2nd row of Panel A, P1] 1(1:2:2:3:3) times, K1, ★ [K1, P1, K1] all in next st, P3 tog ★; rep from ★ to ★ 1(3:4:4:3:4) times more, K1(2:0:3:0:2).

**3rd row** P10(19:21:24:17:23), K1 tbl, [work 3rd row of Panel A, K1 tbl] 1(1:2:2:3:3) times, work 3rd row of Panel B, K1 tbl, work 3rd row of Panel A, P1.

**4th row** K1, work 4th row of Panel A, P1, work 4th row of Panel B, P1, [work 4th row of Panel A, P1] 1(1:2:2:3:3) times, K1, ★ P3 tog, [K1, P1, K1] all in next st ★; rep from ★ to ★ 1(3:4:4:3:4) times more, K1(2:0:3:0:2).

These 4 rows set patt. Cont in patt as set, working appropriate rows of Panels until work measures 12(12:14:15:15:15)cm/4¾(4¾:5½:6:6:6)in from beg, ending with a wrong side row.

### *Place Pocket*

**Next row** Patt 21(30:33:36:40:46), sl next 20(20:30:30:30:30) sts onto a holder, patt across sts of one pocket lining, patt to end. ★★★★
Cont in patt across all sts until work measures 35(43:56:57:58:60)cm/13¾(17:22:22½:23:23½)in from beg, ending with a wrong side row.

### *Shape Neck*

Keeping patt correct, cast off 5(6:5:6:6:6) sts at beg of next row and 1(1:2:2:2:2) foll alt rows. Dec one st at neck edge on every row until 36(43:53:55:58:63) sts rem.
Cont without shaping for a few rows until work measures same as Back to shoulder shaping, ending at side edge. Cast off.

### RIGHT FRONT

Work as given for Left Front to ★★★.
Change to 4½mm (No 7/US 8) needles. Work in patt as follows:

**1st row (right side)** P1, work 1st row of Panel A, K1 tbl, work 1st row of Panel B, K1 tbl, [work 1st row of Panel A, K1 tbl] 1(1:2:2:3:3) times, P to end.

**2nd row** K1(2:0:3:0:2), ★ [K1, P1, K1] all in next st, P3 tog ★; rep from ★ to ★ 1(3:4:4:3:4) times more, K1, P1, [work 2nd row of Panel A, P1] 1(1:2:2:3:3) times, work 2nd row of Panel B, P1, work 2nd row of Panel A, K1.

**3rd row** P1, work 3rd row of Panel A, K1 tbl, work 3rd row of Panel B, K1 tbl, [work 3rd row of Panel A, K1 tbl] 1(1:2:2:3:3) times, P to end.

**4th row** K1(2:0:3:0:2), ★ P3 tog, [K1, P1, K1] all in next st ★; rep from ★ to ★ 1(3:4:4:3:4) times more, K1, P1, [work 4th row of Panel A, P1] 1(1:2:2:3:3) times, work 4th row of Panel B, P1, work 4th row of Panel A, K1.

These 4 rows set patt. Cont in patt as set, working appropriate rows of Panels until work measures 12(12:14:15:15:15)cm/4¾(4¾:5½:6: 6:6)in from beg, ending with a wrong side row.

### Place Pocket

**Next row** Patt 11, sl next 20(20:30:30:30:30) sts onto a holder, patt across sts of one pocket lining, patt to end. ★★★★★

Complete to match Left Front, reversing neck shaping.

### SLEEVES

With 3¾mm (No 9/US 6) needles cast on 33(35:39:41:45:47) sts.

Work in rib as given for Back for 6(6:6:7:7:7)cm/ 2½(2½:2½:2¾:2¾:2¾)in, ending with a right side row.

**Next row** Rib 2(4:4:2:4:4), inc in each st to last 2(4:4:2:4:4) sts, rib to end. 62(62:70:78:82:86) sts.

Change to 4½mm (No 7/US 8) needles. Work in patt as follows:

**1st row (right side)** P10(10:14:18:20:22), K1 tbl, work 1st row of Panel A, K1 tbl, work 1st row of Panel B, K1 tbl, work 1st row of Panel A, K1 tbl, P to end.

**2nd row** K1(1:1:1:3:1), ★ [K1, P1, K1] all in next st, P3 tog ★; rep from ★ to ★ 1(1:2:3:3:4) times more, K1, P1, work 2nd row of Panel A, P1, work 2nd row of Panel B, P1, work 2nd row of Panel A, P1, K1, rep from ★ to ★ 2(2:3:4:4:5) times, K1(1:1:1:3:1).

**3rd row** P10(10:14:18:20:22), K1 tbl, work 3rd row of Panel A, K1 tbl, work 3rd row of Panel B, K1 tbl, work 3rd row of Panel A, K1 tbl, P to end.

**4th row** K1(1:1:1:3:1), ★ P3 tog, [K1, P1, K1] all in next st ★; rep from ★ to ★ 1(1:2:3:3:4) times more, K1, P1, work 4th row of Panel A, P1, work 4th row of Panel B, P1, work 4th row of Panel A, P1, K1, rep from ★ to ★ 2(2:3:4:4:5) times, K1(1:1:1:3:1).

These 4 rows set patt. Cont in patt as set, working appropriate rows of Panels, **at the same time**, inc one st at each end of next and every foll 4th(4th:3rd:3rd:3rd:3rd) row until there are 82(90:114:124:130:136) sts, working inc sts into side edge patt.

Cont without shaping until work measures 27(34:42:44:45:47)cm/10½(13¼:16½:17¼:17¾: 18½)in from beg, ending with a wrong side row.

### Shape Saddle

Cast off 31(35:47:52:55:58) sts at beg of next 2 rows. Cont in patt on rem 20 sts until saddle, when slightly stretched, fits across Front shoulder, ending with a wrong side row. Cast off.

### POCKET TOPS

With 3¾mm (No 9/US 6) needles and right side facing, K across sts of one pocket top dec one st at centre. 19(19:29:29:29:29) sts. Beg with a 2nd row, work 5 rows in rib as given for Back. Cast off in rib.

### NECKBAND

Sew on sleeves, sewing row ends of saddles to shoulders on Back and Fronts.

With 3¾mm (No 9/US 6) needles and right side facing, pick up and K 13(15:18:19:20:21) sts up right front neck, 16 sts across right saddle, K across 31(35:41:43:45:47) sts on back neck dec 4 sts evenly, pick up and K 16 sts across left saddle and 13(15:18:19:20:21) sts down left front neck. 85(93:105:109:113:117) sts. Beg with a 2nd row, work 8 rows in rib as given for Back. Cast off in rib.

## BUTTONHOLE BAND

With 3¾mm (No 9/US 6) needles and right side facing, pick up and K 85(103:133:135:137: 145) sts evenly along front edge of Right Front *for her* or Left Front *for him* (including neckband). Beg with a 2nd row, work 3 rows in rib as given for Back.

**1st buttonhole row** Rib 3(3:3:4:4:4), [cast off 2, rib until there are 11(14:16:16:14:15) sts on right-hand needle] to last 4(4:4:5:5:5) sts, cast off 2, rib to end.

**2nd buttonhole row** Rib to end, casting on 2 sts over those cast off in previous row.
Work 3 rows in rib. Cast off in rib.

## BUTTON BAND

Work to match Buttonhole Band omitting buttonholes.

## TO MAKE UP

Join side and sleeve seams. Catch down pocket linings and sides of pocket tops. Sew on buttons.

## *V NECK CARDIGAN*

### BACK AND POCKET LININGS

Work as given for Back and Pocket Linings of Round Neck Cardigan.

### LEFT FRONT

Work as given for Left Front of Round Neck Cardigan to ★★★★.
Cont in patt across all sts until work measures 26(32:41:41:42:43)cm/10¼(12½:16:16:16½:17)in from beg, ending with a wrong side row.

#### *Shape Front*

Keeping patt correct, dec one st at end (front edge) of next and every alt row until 36(43:53: 55:58:63) sts rem.
Cont without shaping until work measures same as Back to shoulder shaping, ending at side edge. Cast off.

### RIGHT FRONT

Work as given for Right Front of Round Neck Cardigan to ★★★★★. Complete to match Left Front, reversing front shaping.

## SLEEVES AND POCKET TOPS

Work as given for Sleeves and Pocket Tops of Round Neck Cardigan.

## FRONT BAND

Sew on sleeves, sewing row ends of saddles to shoulders on Back and Fronts.
With 3¾mm (No 9/US 6) circular needle and right side facing, pick up and K 60(75:91:91:93:97) sts up straight front edge of Right Front, 32(37:48:50:50:53) sts up shaped edge, 16 sts across right saddle, K across 31(35:41:43:45:47) sts on back neck dec 4 sts evenly, pick up and K 16 sts across left saddle, 32(37:48:50:50:53) sts down shaped edge of Left Front and 60(75:91:91:93:97) sts down straight front edge. 243(287:347:353:359:375) sts. Work backwards and forwards. Beg with a 2nd row, work 3 rows in rib as given for Back of Round Neck Cardigan.

**1st buttonhole row** *For her:* Rib 2(2:3:3:4:3), ★[cast off 2, rib until there are 9(12:12:12:12:13) sts on right-hand needle] 5(5:6:6:6:6) times, cast off 2, rib to end. *For him:* Rib to last 59(74:89:89:90:95) sts, work as given *for her* from ★ to end.

**2nd buttonhole row** Rib to end, casting on 2 sts over those cast off in previous row.
Work 3 rows in rib. Cast off in rib.

## TO MAKE UP

Join side and sleeve seams. Catch down pocket linings and sides of pocket tops. Sew on buttons.

## MATERIALS

13(14) 100g balls of Hayfield Brig Aran.
1 pair in each of 3¾mm (No 9/US 4)
and 4½mm (No 7/US 6) knitting
needles.
One 3¾mm (No 9/US 4) circular
needle, 50cm long.
Cable needle.

## MEASUREMENTS

To fit chest 97–107(112-122)cm
38-42(44-48)in
All round at chest 118(134)cm
46½(52¾)in
Length to shoulder 69cm/27in
Sleeve seam 52cm/20½in

## TENSION

26 sts and 26 rows to 10cm/4in square
measured over patt on 4½mm (No 7/
US 6) needles.

## ABBREVIATIONS

Cr3R-sl next 2 sts onto cable needle and
leave at back, K1 tbl, sl first (P) st on
cable needle back onto left-hand needle
and P this st, then K1 tbl from cable
needle.
C3-sl next 2 sts onto cable needle and
leave at back, K1 tbl, then K2 tbl from
cable needle.
Cr2L-sl next st onto cable needle and
leave at front, P1, then K1 tbl from cable
needle.
Cr2R-sl next st onto cable needle and
leave at back, K1 tbl, then P1 from cable
needle.
C2B-sl next st onto cable needle and
leave at back, K1 tbl, then K1 tbl from
cable needle.
C2F-sl next st onto cable needle and
leave at front, K1 tbl, then K1 tbl from
cable needle.
Also see page 8.

# TWISTED RIB ARAN SWEATER

## PANEL A

### WORKED OVER 41 STS

**1st row (wrong side)** [K1, P1 tbl] 7 times, K5,
P3 tbl, K5, [P1 tbl, K1] 7 times.
**2nd row** [P1, K1 tbl] 4 times, [Cr2R] 3 times,
P5, C3, P5, [Cr2L] 3 times, [K1 tbl, P1] 4 times.
**3rd row** [K1, P1 tbl] 4 times, [P1 tbl, K1] 3
times, K5, P3 tbl, K5, [K1, P1 tbl] 3 times, [P1
tbl, K1] 4 times.
**4th row** [P1, K1 tbl] 3 times, P1, [Cr2R] 3
times, P5, Cr2R, K1 tbl, Cr2L, P5, [Cr2L] 3
times, P1, [K1 tbl, P1] 3 times.
**5th row** [K1, P1 tbl] 6 times, K6, [P1 tbl, K1]
3 times, K5, [P1 tbl, K1] 6 times.
**6th row** [P1, K1 tbl] 3 times, [Cr2R] 3 times,
P5, C2B, P1, K1 tbl, P1, C2F, P5, [Cr2L] 3
times, [K1 tbl, P1] 3 times.
**7th row** [K1, P1 tbl] 3 times, [P1 tbl, K1] 3
times, K5, P2 tbl, K1, P1 tbl, K1, P2 tbl, K5,
[K1, P1 tbl] 3 times, [P1 tbl, K1] 3 times.
**8th row** [P1, K1 tbl] twice, P1, [Cr2R] 3 times,
P5, Cr2R, K1 tbl, [P1, K1 tbl] twice, Cr2L,
P5, [Cr2L] 3 times, P1, [K1 tbl, P1] twice.
**9th row** [K1, P1 tbl] 5 times, K6, [P1 tbl, K1]
5 times, K5, [P1 tbl, K1] 5 times.
**10th row** [P1, K1 tbl] twice, [Cr2R] 3 times,
P5, C2B, P1, [K1 tbl, P1] 3 times, C2F, P5,
[Cr2L] 3 times, [K1 tbl, P1] twice.
**11th row** [K1, P1 tbl] twice, [P1 tbl, K1] 3
times, K5, P2 tbl, [K1, P1 tbl] 4 times, P1 tbl,
K5, [K1, P1 tbl] 3 times, [P1 tbl, K1] twice.
**12th row** P1, K1 tbl, P1, [Cr2R] 3 times, P5,
Cr2R, K1 tbl, [P1, K1 tbl] 4 times, Cr2L, P5,
[Cr2L] 3 times, P1, K1 tbl, P1.
**13th row** [K1, P1 tbl] 4 times, K6, [P1 tbl, K1]
7 times, K5, [P1 tbl, K1] 4 times.
**14th row** P1, K1 tbl, [Cr2R] 3 times, P5, C2B,
P1, [K1 tbl, P1] 5 times, C2F, P5, [Cr2L] 3
times, K1 tbl, P1.
**15th row** K1, P1 tbl, [P1 tbl, K1] 3 times, K5,
P2 tbl, [K1, P1 tbl] 6 times, P1 tbl, K5, [K1,
P1 tbl] 3 times, P1 tbl, K1.
**16th row** P1, [Cr2R] 3 times, P5, Cr2R, K1
tbl, [P1, K1 tbl] 6 times, Cr2L, P5, [Cr2L] 3
times, P1.
**17th row** [K1, P1 tbl] 3 times, K6, [P1 tbl, K1]
9 times, K5, [P1 tbl, K1] 3 times.

**18th row** P1, C2F, [Cr2L] twice, P5, Cr2L, K1 tbl, [P1, K1 tbl] 6 times, Cr2R, P5, [Cr2R] twice, C2B, P1.

**19th row** As 15th row.

**20th row** P1, K1 tbl, [Cr2L] 3 times, P5, Cr2L, P1, [K1 tbl, P1] 5 times, Cr2R, P5, [Cr2R] 3 times, K1 tbl, P1.

**21st row** As 13th row.

**22nd row** P1, K1 tbl, P1, C2F, [Cr2L] twice, P5, Cr2L, K1 tbl, [P1, K1 tbl] 4 times, Cr2R, P5, [Cr2R] twice, C2B, P1, K1 tbl, P1.

**23rd row** As 11th row.

**24th row** [P1, K1 tbl] twice, [Cr2L] 3 times, P5, Cr2L, P1, [K1 tbl, P1] 3 times, Cr2R, P5, [Cr2R] 3 times, [K1 tbl, P1] twice.

**25th row** As 9th row.

**26th row** [P1, K1 tbl] twice, P1, C2F, [Cr2L] twice, P5, Cr2L, K1 tbl, [P1, K1 tbl] twice, Cr2R, P5, [Cr2R] twice, C2B, P1, [K1 tbl, P1] twice.

**27th row** As 7th row.

**28th row** [P1, K1 tbl] 3 times, [Cr2L] 3 times, P5, Cr2L, P1, K1 tbl, P1, Cr2R, P5, [Cr2R] 3 times, [K1 tbl, P1] 3 times.

**29th row** As 5th row.

**30th row** [P1, K1 tbl] 3 times, P1, C2F, [Cr2L] twice, P5, Cr2L, K1 tbl, Cr2R, P5, [Cr2R] twice, C2B, P1, [K1 tbl, P1] 3 times.

**31st row** As 3rd row.

**32nd row** [P1, K1 tbl] 4 times, [Cr2L] 3 times, P5, C3, P5, [Cr2R] 3 times, [K1 tbl, P1] 4 times.
These 32 rows form patt.

### PANEL B
WORKED OVER 4 STS

**1st row (wrong side)** P4.

**2nd row** K4.

**3rd row** P4.

**4th row** Sl next 2 sts onto cable needle and leave at back, K2, then K2 from cable needle.
These 4 rows form patt.

### PANEL C
WORKED OVER 7 STS

**1st row (wrong side)** K1, P1 tbl, K3, P1 tbl, K1.

**2nd row** P1, K1 tbl, P3, K1 tbl, P1.

**3rd row** As 1st row.

**4th to 7th rows** Rep 2nd and 3rd rows twice.

**8th row** P1, Cr2L, P1, Cr2R, P1.

**9th row** K2, P1 tbl, K1, P1 tbl, K2.

**10th row** P2, Cr3R, P2.

**11th row** As 9th row.

**12th row** P1, Cr2R, P1, Cr2L, P1.

**13th to 16th rows** Rep 1st and 2nd rows twice.
These 16 rows form patt.

### BACK

With 3¾mm (No 9/US 4) needles cast on 133(145) sts.

Work in rib patt as follows:

**1st row (right side)** * K2, [P1, K1 tbl] 4 times, P1, K1; rep from * to last st, K1.

**2nd row** * P2, [K1, P1 tbl] 4 times, K1, P1; rep from * to last st, P1.

**3rd to 6th rows** Rep 1st and 2nd rows twice.

**7th row** * K2, P1, sl next 4 sts onto cable needle and leave at back, K1 tbl, P1, K1 tbl, then [P1, K1 tbl] twice from cable needle, P1, K1; rep from * to last st, K1.

**8th row** As 2nd row.

These 8 rows form rib patt. Work a further 26 rows in rib patt.

**Next row** P4(7), * P twice in next st, P6(4), P twice in next st, P5(3); rep from * to last 12 sts, [P twice in next st, P5] twice. 153(175) sts. Change to 4½mm (No 7/US 6) needles. Work in main patt as follows:

**1st row (wrong side)** Work 1st row of Panel A (C), [work 1st row of Panel B, Panel C(A), Panel B, then Panel A(C)] 2(3) times.

**2nd row** Work 2nd row of Panel A(C), [work 2nd row of Panel B, Panel C(A), Panel B, then Panel A(C)] 2(3) times.

These 2 rows set main patt. Cont in main patt, working appropriate rows of Panels until work measures 69cm/27in from beg, ending with a wrong side row.

### Shape Shoulders
**Next row** Cast off 52(61) sts, patt to last 52(61) sts, cast off these sts. Leave rem 49(53) sts on a holder.

## FRONT

Work as given for Back until work measures 59cm/23¼in from beg, ending with a wrong side row.

### Shape Neck
**Next row** Patt 59(68), turn. Work on this set of sts only.

Keeping patt correct, dec one st at neck edge on next 4 rows, then on 3 foll alt rows. 52(61) sts.

Cont without shaping until work measures same as Back to shoulder shaping, ending with a wrong side row. Cast off.

With right side facing, sl centre 35(39) sts onto a holder, rejoin yarn to rem sts and patt to end. Complete to match first side.

## SLEEVES

With 3¾mm (No 9/US 4) needles cast on 61 sts.

Beg with a 1st row, work 26 rows in rib patt as given for Back.

**Next row** P3, [P twice in next st, P5] 9 times, P twice in next st, P3. 71 sts.

Change to 4½mm (No 7/US 6) needles. Work in main patt as follows:

**1st row (wrong side)** Work 1st row of Panel B, Panel C, Panel B, Panel A, Panel B, Panel C and Panel B.

**2nd row** Work 2nd row of Panel B, Panel C, Panel B, Panel A, Panel B, Panel C and Panel B.

These 2 rows set main patt. Cont in main patt, working appropriate rows of Panels, **at the same time**, inc one st at each end of next and every foll 3rd row until there are 131 sts, working inc sts into main patt.

Cont without shaping until work measures

52cm/20½in from beg, ending with a wrong side row. Cast off.

## NECKBAND

Join shoulder seams.

With 3¾mm (No 9/US 4) circular needle and right side facing, pick up and K22 sts down left front neck, K across 35(39) sts at centre front, pick up and K22 sts up right front neck, K across 49(53) back neck sts. 128(136) sts. Work in rounds. P 1 round.

**1st to 3rd rounds** ★ P1, [K1 tbl, P1] twice, K3; rep from ★ to end.

**4th round** ★ P1, Cr3R, P1, K3; rep from ★ to end.

Rep these 4 rounds 4 times more, then work 1st round again.

**Next round** ★ K1, K3 tog, K4; rep from ★ to end. 96(102) sts.

K 4 rounds. Cast off.

## TO MAKE UP

Sew on sleeves, placing centre of sleeves to shoulder seams. Join side and sleeve seams.